I0465342

Email Marketing

A Comprehensive Guide to Strategies, Tips, and Best Practices for Effective Email Campaigns for Drive Sales, Build Relationships, Increased Sales and Grow Your Business

Lewis Finan

Copyright 2024 by Lewis Finan - All rights reserved.

This document is geared towards providing exact and reliable information in regards to the topic and issue covered. The publication is sold with the idea that the publisher is not required to render accounting, officially permitted, or otherwise, qualified services. If advice is necessary, legal or professional, a practiced individual in the profession should be ordered.

-        From a Declaration of Principles which was accepted and approved equally by a Committee of the American Bar Association and a Committee of Publishers and Associations.

In no way is it legal to reproduce, duplicate, or transmit any part of this document in either electronic means or in printed format. Recording of this publication is strictly prohibited and any storage of this document is not allowed unless with written permission from the publisher. All rights reserved.

The information provided herein is stated to be truthful and consistent, in that any liability, in terms of inattention or otherwise, by any usage or abuse of any policies, processes, or directions contained within is the solitary and utter responsibility of the recipient reader. Under no circumstances will any legal responsibility or blame be held against the publisher for any reparation, damages, or monetary loss due to the information herein, either directly or indirectly.

Respective authors own all copyrights not held by the publisher.

The information herein is offered for informational purposes solely, and is universal as so.

The presentation of the information is without contract or any type of guarantee assurance.

The trademarks that are used are without any consent, and the publication of the trademark is without permission or backing by the trademark owner. All trademarks and brands within this book are for clarifying purposes only and are the owned by the owners themselves, not affiliated with this document.

Table of Contents

Introduction:

Welcome to "Email Marketing: A Comprehensive Guide to Strategies, Tips, and Best Practices for Effective Email Campaigns to Drive Sales, Build Relationships, and Grow Your Business."

In today's digital age, email remains one of the most powerful and cost-effective tools for businesses to connect with their audience, drive sales, and foster lasting relationships. With its unparalleled reach and direct line of communication, email marketing continues to be a cornerstone of successful marketing strategies across industries.

However, mastering email marketing requires more than just sending out occasional newsletters or promotional blasts. It demands a deep understanding of your audience, thoughtful strategy, and adherence to best practices. That's where this comprehensive guide comes in.

Whether you're a seasoned marketer looking to enhance your email campaigns or a business owner seeking to unlock the full potential of email marketing, this guide is designed to provide you with the knowledge and tools necessary to succeed.

Throughout the following chapters, we'll explore every facet of email marketing, from laying a strong foundation and crafting compelling campaigns to implementing advanced techniques and staying ahead of emerging trends. You'll learn how to set clear goals, segment your audience effectively, create engaging content, and leverage automation to streamline your efforts.

Real-world examples and case studies will illustrate key concepts and offer actionable insights, while discussions on deliverability, compliance, and analytics will ensure that your campaigns not only reach your audience but also deliver measurable results.

Whether you're a small business looking to build your brand or a large corporation aiming to optimize your email strategy, this guide is your roadmap to success in the ever-evolving landscape of email marketing.

So, let's dive in and unlock the full potential of email marketing together. By implementing the strategies, tips, and best practices outlined in this guide, you'll be well on your way to driving sales, building meaningful relationships, and growing your business through the power of email.

Chapter 1: Introduction to Email Marketing

In the bustling digital landscape of the 21st century, where attention spans are fleeting and competition is fierce, email marketing stands out as a beacon of opportunity for businesses large and small. In this chapter, we embark on a journey to unravel the intricacies of email marketing, exploring its evolution, significance, and unparalleled potential in today's business realm.

The Genesis of Email Marketing

To understand the essence of email marketing, we must first trace its origins back to the dawn of the Internet age. Picture the early 1970s, a time when ARPANET, the precursor to the internet, was in its nascent stages. Amidst the exchange of scientific data and academic discourse, an innovation was brewing - the birth of electronic mail, or email.

Initially conceived as a means of facilitating communication between researchers and academics, email swiftly permeated various spheres of society. As the digital landscape burgeoned, so did the utility of email, transcending geographical barriers and revolutionizing the way individuals connected and communicated.

The Evolution of Email Marketing

Fast forward to the advent of the commercial internet in the 1990s, and email marketing emerged as a powerful tool for businesses to engage with their audience on a personal level. With the proliferation of email service providers and the development of user-friendly interfaces, businesses seized the opportunity to harness the potential of email as a marketing channel.

From rudimentary text-based messages to visually captivating HTML emails, the evolution of email marketing mirrored the technological advancements of the digital era. With the advent of automation and analytics, marketers gained unprecedented insights into consumer behavior, enabling them to tailor their campaigns with precision and finesse.

The Significance of Email Marketing

In an age inundated with an array of digital marketing channels, one might ponder the enduring relevance of email marketing. The answer lies in its unparalleled efficacy as a direct and intimate means of communication. Unlike social media or search engine marketing, where algorithms dictate visibility, email marketing affords marketers a direct line to their audience's inbox.

Moreover, email marketing boasts an impressive return on investment (ROI), outperforming other digital marketing channels in terms of cost-effectiveness and conversion rates. Whether nurturing leads, promoting products, or fostering brand loyalty, email marketing serves as a versatile tool in the marketer's arsenal.

The Unparalleled Potential

As we embark on this exploration of email marketing, it becomes abundantly clear that its potential knows no bounds. From startups seeking to establish their presence to multinational corporations aiming to cultivate customer loyalty, email marketing offers a myriad of opportunities for businesses of all sizes.

In the chapters that follow, we delve deeper into the nuances of email marketing, exploring strategies, best practices, and case studies that illustrate its transformative power. As we unravel the intricacies of segmentation, personalization, and engagement, we equip ourselves with the tools to navigate the ever-evolving landscape of digital marketing.

In conclusion, email marketing transcends the realm of mere marketing; it embodies the art of forging genuine connections, nurturing relationships, and captivating hearts and minds. Join me on this journey as we unravel the tapestry of email marketing, weaving together threads of innovation, creativity, and human connection.

1.1 What is Email Marketing?

Email marketing is a dynamic and versatile digital marketing strategy that revolves around the strategic use of email communication to engage with audiences, nurture relationships, and drive business objectives. At its core, email marketing involves the creation and dissemination of targeted email messages to a specific group of recipients to achieve various marketing goals.

Evolution and Importance

The origins of email marketing can be traced back to the early days of the internet when electronic mail emerged as a revolutionary communication tool. Initially used for personal correspondence, email quickly evolved into a powerful marketing channel as businesses recognized its potential to reach customers directly and cost-effectively.

Over the years, email marketing has undergone significant evolution, adapting to technological advancements and changing consumer behaviors. From simple text-based messages to sophisticated, visually appealing campaigns, the scope and capabilities of email marketing have expanded exponentially.

Key Components

Effective email marketing campaigns comprise several key components, each playing a vital role in achieving success:

- **Target Audience**: Identifying and segmenting the target audience based on demographics, interests, and behaviors is crucial for crafting personalized and relevant email content.
- **Content**: Compelling and engaging content lies at the heart of email marketing. Whether it's promotional offers, informative newsletters, or educational resources, the content should resonate with the audience and align with the brand's messaging.
- **Design**: Visual appeal plays a significant role in capturing the recipient's attention. Well-designed emails with clear calls-to-action and mobile responsiveness enhance the user experience and drive engagement.
- **Automation**: Automation tools allow marketers to streamline the email marketing process, from welcome emails to drip campaigns and abandoned cart reminders. Automation enables timely and personalized communication at scale, maximizing efficiency and effectiveness.

- **Analytics**: Tracking and analyzing key metrics such as open rates, click-through rates, and conversion rates provide valuable insights into campaign performance. Data-driven decision-making allows marketers to optimize their strategies and achieve better results over time.

Benefits and Challenges

Email marketing offers a plethora of benefits for businesses:

- **Cost-effectiveness**: Compared to traditional marketing channels, email marketing is relatively inexpensive, making it accessible to businesses of all sizes.
- **Direct communication**: Email provides a direct line of communication to the recipient's inbox, enabling personalized interactions and fostering customer relationships.
- **Measurable results**: Robust analytics tools allow marketers to track the performance of their campaigns in real time, enabling optimization and continuous improvement.

However, email marketing also presents certain challenges, including deliverability issues, spam filters, and maintaining subscriber engagement. Overcoming these challenges requires a strategic approach, ongoing experimentation, and a commitment to delivering value to the audience.

In conclusion, email marketing remains a cornerstone of modern marketing strategies, offering unparalleled opportunities for businesses to connect with their audience, drive engagement, and achieve their marketing objectives. By leveraging the power of targeted communication, compelling content, and data-driven insights, businesses can harness the full potential of email marketing to foster brand loyalty, drive conversions, and propel growth in an increasingly digital world.

1.2 The Evolution and Importance of Email Marketing

In the ever-evolving landscape of digital marketing, email marketing has emerged as a cornerstone strategy, evolving from its humble beginnings to becoming a powerful tool for businesses worldwide. This chapter delves into the evolution of email marketing and its enduring significance in today's marketing ecosystem.

Evolution of Email Marketing

The genesis of email marketing can be traced back to the early days of the Internet, where email served as a means of interpersonal communication. As businesses recognized the potential of email to reach a broader audience, rudimentary marketing messages began to surface, albeit with limited sophistication.

Throughout the 1990s and early 2000s, email marketing underwent rapid evolution fueled by technological advancements and shifting consumer behaviors. The introduction of HTML email enabled marketers to craft visually captivating messages, while the proliferation of email service providers facilitated mass distribution and tracking capabilities.

The advent of automation further revolutionized email marketing, empowering marketers to deliver personalized and timely messages at scale. From automated welcome sequences to behavior-triggered campaigns, automation has streamlined the email marketing process, enhancing efficiency and effectiveness.

Importance of Email Marketing

In today's digital age, email marketing remains as relevant and impactful as ever, owing to several key factors:

- **Direct Communication**: Email provides a direct line of communication to the recipient's inbox, allowing businesses to engage with their audience on a personal level. Unlike social media or display advertising, email marketing offers a controlled environment free from algorithmic constraints.
- **Cost-Effectiveness**: Compared to traditional marketing channels such as print or television advertising, email marketing is highly cost-effective. With minimal overhead costs and the ability to reach a large audience at a fraction of the cost, email marketing delivers an impressive return on investment (ROI).
- **Targeted Approach**: Email marketing enables businesses to segment their audience based on demographics, behaviors, and preferences, allowing for highly targeted and relevant messaging. By delivering personalized content to the right audience segments, businesses can increase engagement and drive conversions.
- **Measurable Results**: Robust analytics tools provide marketers with valuable insights into the performance of their email campaigns. Metrics such as open rates, click-through rates, and conversion rates enable data-driven decision-making, allowing marketers to optimize their strategies for maximum impact.

In conclusion, the evolution of email marketing from its humble beginnings to its current state as a sophisticated and indispensable marketing tool is a testament to its enduring significance. By leveraging the power of direct communication, personalization, and data-driven insights, businesses can harness the full potential of email marketing to engage with their audience, drive conversions, and achieve their marketing objectives in an increasingly competitive digital landscape.

1.3 Key Benefits of Email Marketing

Email marketing stands out as a versatile and indispensable tool in the marketer's arsenal, offering a multitude of benefits for businesses of all sizes. In this section, we explore the key advantages of email marketing and how it can help businesses achieve their marketing objectives effectively.

1. Cost-Effectiveness

One of the most significant advantages of email marketing is its cost-effectiveness. Unlike traditional marketing channels such as print or television advertising, which require substantial financial investment, email marketing can be executed at a fraction of the cost. With minimal overhead expenses and no printing or postage fees, email campaigns offer an impressive return on investment (ROI) for businesses, making it accessible even for those with limited marketing budgets.

2. Direct Communication

Email marketing provides businesses with a direct line of communication to their audience's inbox. Unlike social media or display advertising, which are subject to algorithmic changes and platform restrictions, email allows businesses to control the delivery and timing of their messages. This direct communication fosters a sense of intimacy and trust between the brand and its audience, enabling personalized interactions and meaningful engagement.

3. Targeted Approach

Another key benefit of email marketing is its ability to target specific segments of the audience with personalized messaging. Through segmentation based on demographics, behaviors, and preferences, businesses can tailor their email campaigns to resonate with different audience segments. By delivering relevant content to the right people at the right time, businesses can increase engagement, drive conversions, and foster long-term customer relationships.

4. Measurable Results

Email marketing offers robust analytics tools that provide valuable insights into campaign performance. Metrics such as open rates, click-through rates, and conversion rates allow marketers to track the effectiveness of their email campaigns in real time. By analyzing these metrics, businesses can identify areas for improvement, optimize their strategies, and achieve better results over time. This data-driven approach enables marketers to make informed decisions and maximize the impact of their email marketing efforts.

5. Increased Brand Awareness and Loyalty

Consistent and strategic email communication helps businesses increase brand awareness and foster customer loyalty. By regularly engaging with their audience through informative content, promotional offers, and personalized recommendations, businesses can reinforce their brand identity and stay top-of-mind with customers. Additionally, email marketing allows businesses to nurture relationships with existing customers, encouraging repeat purchases and advocacy, thus strengthening brand loyalty over time.

6. Scalability and Flexibility

Email marketing is highly scalable and adaptable to the needs of businesses of all sizes. Whether you're a small startup or a multinational corporation, email marketing can be tailored to suit your objectives, budget, and resources. With the ability to automate processes, segment audiences, and personalize content, businesses can scale their email marketing efforts as they grow and evolve, ensuring continued success and relevance in a dynamic marketplace.

In conclusion, email marketing offers a plethora of benefits for businesses seeking to engage with their audience, drive conversions, and achieve their marketing goals. From cost-effectiveness and direct communication to targeted messaging and measurable results, email marketing remains a cornerstone of modern marketing strategies, empowering businesses to connect with their audience in meaningful and impactful ways.

1.4 Overview of Email Marketing Metrics

Email marketing metrics play a crucial role in assessing the effectiveness of email campaigns and informing strategic decision-making. In this section, we provide an overview of the key metrics used to measure the performance of email marketing campaigns and their significance in evaluating success.

1. Open Rate

The open rate is a fundamental metric that measures the percentage of recipients who open an email out of the total number of emails delivered. A high open rate indicates that the subject line and preview text resonated with the audience, enticing them to engage with the email content. Factors influencing open rates include the relevance of the subject line, the sender's reputation, and the timing of the email.

2. Click-Through Rate (CTR)

The click-through rate measures the percentage of recipients who clicked on a link or call-to-action (CTA) within the email. It provides insights into the effectiveness of the email content and the clarity of the CTA. A high CTR indicates that the email successfully engaged recipients and motivated them to take action. Factors affecting CTR include the relevance of the content, placement, and visibility of links, and the design of the email.

3. Conversion Rate

The conversion rate measures the percentage of recipients who completed a desired action, such as making a purchase, signing up for a newsletter, or filling out a form, after clicking on a link within the email. It is a key indicator of the email's impact on driving desired outcomes and achieving business objectives. Factors influencing conversion rates include the relevance of the offer, ease of completing the desired action, and alignment with recipient preferences.

4. Bounce Rate

The bounce rate measures the percentage of emails that were not successfully delivered to recipients' inboxes due to reasons such as invalid email addresses, server issues, or spam filters. Bounces are categorized as either "hard bounces," which are permanent delivery failures, or "soft bounces," which are temporary issues that may be resolved upon subsequent delivery attempts. Monitoring bounce rates helps maintain a clean and healthy email list and ensures deliverability to engaged recipients.

5. Unsubscribe Rate

The unsubscribe rate measures the percentage of recipients who opt out of receiving future emails from a sender after receiving a particular email campaign. While some level of unsubscribes is natural, a high unsubscribe rate may indicate issues with email frequency, relevance, or content quality. Monitoring unsubscribe rates allows marketers to identify potential areas for improvement and refine their email marketing strategies to better align with recipient preferences.

6. Engagement Metrics

Engagement metrics, such as the time spent reading an email, the number of shares or forwards, and the interaction with multimedia content (e.g., videos or interactive elements), provide insights into recipients' level of engagement with the email content. These metrics go beyond traditional open and click-through rates to measure the depth of audience interaction and the effectiveness of the email in capturing attention and driving engagement.

In summary, email marketing metrics serve as valuable tools for evaluating the performance of email campaigns, identifying areas for improvement, and optimizing strategies for maximum impact. By monitoring key metrics and iteratively refining their approach, marketers can enhance the effectiveness of their email marketing efforts and achieve their business objectives more effectively.

Chapter 2: Building a Quality Email List

In the realm of email marketing, success begins with the foundation - a quality email list. Building an email list comprised of engaged and receptive subscribers is essential for achieving long-term success and maximizing the impact of your email campaigns. In this chapter, we explore the strategies and best practices for building a quality email list that drives results and fosters meaningful connections with your audience.

Understanding the Importance of a Quality Email List

Before delving into the strategies for building a quality email list, it's crucial to understand why it matters. A quality email list serves as the lifeblood of your email marketing efforts, providing a pool of engaged subscribers who have willingly opted in to receive communications from your brand. Unlike purchased or rented email lists, which often result in low engagement and high unsubscribe rates, a quality email list consists of individuals who are genuinely interested in your products, services, or content.

Building a quality email list enables you to:

- **Nurture Relationships**: By cultivating a list of engaged subscribers, you can nurture relationships with your audience, fostering trust, loyalty, and brand advocacy over time.

- **Increase Engagement**: Engaged subscribers are more likely to open, click, and interact with your email campaigns, driving higher engagement rates and ultimately, better results.
- **Enhance Deliverability**: Email service providers prioritize delivering emails to engaged subscribers' inboxes, helping to maintain high deliverability rates and avoid being flagged as spam.
- **Maximize ROI**: A quality email list yields higher returns on investment (ROI) by enabling more targeted and relevant communication, resulting in increased conversions and revenue generation.

Strategies for Building a Quality Email List

Now that we've established the importance of a quality email list, let's explore the strategies and tactics for building and growing your subscriber base:

1. Offer Valuable Incentives

Entice visitors to subscribe to your email list by offering valuable incentives such as:

- **Lead Magnets**: Create compelling lead magnets such as ebooks, whitepapers, or exclusive content that provide value to your audience in exchange for their email address.
- **Discounts or Promotions**: Offer exclusive discounts, promotions, or freebies to new subscribers as a token of appreciation for joining your list.

- **Contests or Giveaways**: Host contests or giveaways where participants can enter by subscribing to your email list, encouraging them to opt in for a chance to win.

2. Optimize Website Sign-Up Forms

Optimize your website's sign-up forms to make it easy for visitors to subscribe to your email list:

- **Placement**: Position sign-up forms prominently on your website, such as in the header, sidebar, footer, or within relevant content.
- **Design**: Design visually appealing and user-friendly sign-up forms that capture attention and encourage conversions.
- **Minimal Fields**: Keep sign-up forms concise by only asking for essential information, such as name and email address, to reduce friction and increase conversions.
- **Clear Call-to-Action (CTA)**: Use clear and compelling CTAs that communicate the value proposition and incentivize visitors to subscribe.

3. Leverage Social Media

Harness the power of social media to expand your email list:

- **Promote Lead Magnets**: Share links to your lead magnets or gated content on social media platforms to attract new subscribers.

- **Host Live Events**: Host live webinars, Q&A sessions, or virtual events and require registration with an email address to participate.
- **Run Social Media Ads**: Launch targeted social media advertising campaigns that drive traffic to dedicated landing pages with sign-up forms.

4. Utilize Content Marketing

Create valuable and engaging content to attract and retain subscribers:

- **Blog Subscriptions**: Offer blog subscriptions to allow readers to receive updates and new content directly in their inboxes.
- **Content Upgrades**: Create content upgrades such as downloadable checklists, templates, or bonus materials that complement your blog posts and require email opt-ins to access.
- **Guest Blogging**: Write guest posts for relevant websites and include a call-to-action directing readers to subscribe to your email list for more content.

5. Implement Referral Programs

Encourage your existing subscribers to refer friends, colleagues, or contacts to join your email list:

- **Referral Incentives**: Offer incentives or rewards to subscribers who refer new sign-ups to your email list, such as discounts, freebies, or exclusive access.

- **Share Buttons**: Include social sharing buttons in your emails to make it easy for subscribers to share your content with their network, extending your reach and potential for new subscribers.

6. Maintain Transparency and Consent

Ensure compliance with data privacy regulations and maintain transparency and consent when collecting email addresses:

- **Opt-In Confirmation**: Implement double opt-in confirmation processes to verify subscriber consent and prevent spam or invalid email addresses.
- **Privacy Policy**: Communicate your privacy policy and how you will use subscribers' information, instilling trust and confidence in your brand.
- **Unsubscribe Options**: Provide easy-to-find unsubscribe options in every email to give subscribers control over their preferences and ensure compliance with unsubscribe regulations.

Building a quality email list is a foundational step in successful email marketing. By implementing strategic tactics and best practices, you can attract, engage, and retain a loyal base of subscribers who eagerly anticipate your emails and actively participate in your campaigns. Remember to focus on providing value, optimizing user experience, and maintaining transparency and consent to create a robust and responsive email list that drives results and fosters meaningful connections with your audience.

2.1 Understanding Your Audience

In the realm of email marketing, success hinges on your ability to understand and connect with your audience on a deeper level. By gaining insights into their needs, preferences, and behaviors, you can tailor your email campaigns to resonate with them effectively. In this section, we explore the importance of understanding your audience and strategies for gaining valuable insights.

Why Understanding Your Audience Matters

Understanding your audience is essential for several reasons:

- **Relevance**: By knowing your audience's interests and preferences, you can create content and offers that resonate with them, increasing engagement and response rates.
- **Personalization**: Understanding your audience allows you to personalize your email campaigns, delivering targeted messages that speak directly to their needs and desires.
- **Retention**: Building strong relationships with your audience fosters loyalty and encourages repeat purchases, ultimately driving long-term retention and customer lifetime value.
- **Optimization**: Insights into your audience's behaviors and preferences enable you to optimize your email marketing strategies, refining your approach to achieve better results over time.

Strategies for Understanding Your Audience

To gain a deeper understanding of your audience, consider implementing the following strategies:

1. Customer Surveys and Feedback

Conduct customer surveys and gather feedback to learn more about your audience's preferences, pain points, and expectations. Use tools such as online surveys, feedback forms, or post-purchase emails to solicit input from your audience and gain valuable insights into their needs and preferences.

2. Audience Segmentation

Segment your email list based on demographic, geographic, psychographic, or behavioral criteria to create targeted and personalized campaigns. By dividing your audience into distinct segments, you can tailor your messaging and offers to better align with their interests and preferences, increasing relevance and engagement.

3. Website and Email Analytics

Utilize website analytics tools such as Google Analytics and email marketing platforms' built-in analytics to track user behavior and engagement metrics. Analyze data such as page views, bounce rates, click-through rates, and conversion rates to gain insights into your audience's interactions with your website and email campaigns, identifying patterns and opportunities for improvement.

4. Social Media Listening

Monitor social media channels and engage in social listening to understand your audience's conversations, sentiments, and interests. Pay attention to comments, reviews, and discussions related to your brand or industry to glean insights into your audience's preferences, pain points, and trends that may impact your email marketing strategy.

5. Customer Interviews and Persona Development

Conduct one-on-one interviews or focus groups with select customers to gain qualitative insights into their motivations, challenges, and behaviors. Use the information gathered to develop buyer personas or customer profiles that represent different segments of your audience, providing a deeper understanding of their needs, preferences, and journeys.

6. Competitive Analysis

Conduct competitive analysis to understand how your competitors are engaging with their audience through email marketing. Evaluate their email content, frequency, promotions, and messaging to identify opportunities to differentiate your brand and better serve your audience's needs and preferences.

Understanding your audience is the cornerstone of effective email marketing. By gaining insights into their needs, preferences, and behaviors, you can create targeted and personalized campaigns that resonate with them on a deeper level, driving engagement, loyalty, and ultimately, business success. By implementing strategies such as customer surveys, audience segmentation, website analytics, social media listening, customer interviews, and competitive analysis, you can gain valuable insights into your audience and optimize your email marketing efforts for maximum impact.

2.2 Effective List-Building Strategies

Building a quality email list is the foundation of successful email marketing. By employing effective list-building strategies, you can attract engaged subscribers who are interested in your brand and eager to receive your communications. In this section, we explore proven strategies for growing your email list and expanding your audience reach.

1. Create Compelling Lead Magnets

Offer valuable incentives, known as lead magnets, to entice visitors to subscribe to your email list. Lead magnets can take various forms, such as:

- **Ebooks or Guides**: Provide in-depth guides, ebooks, or whitepapers that offer valuable insights, tips, or solutions to your audience's pain points.

- **Checklists or Templates**: Offer practical tools such as checklists, templates, or worksheets that help your audience achieve specific goals or tasks.
- **Webinars or Courses**: Host live or recorded webinars, workshops, or courses on topics relevant to your audience's interests or challenges.
- **Exclusive Content**: Offer access to exclusive content, behind-the-scenes updates, or members-only resources that provide added value to your subscribers.

2. Optimize Website Sign-Up Forms

Optimize your website's sign-up forms to make it easy for visitors to subscribe to your email list:

- **Placement**: Position sign-up forms prominently on your website, such as in the header, sidebar, footer, or within relevant content.
- **Design**: Design visually appealing and user-friendly sign-up forms that capture attention and encourage conversions.
- **Minimal Fields**: Keep sign-up forms concise by only asking for essential information, such as name and email address, to reduce friction and increase conversions.
- **Clear Call-to-Action (CTA)**: Use clear and compelling CTAs that communicate the value proposition and incentivize visitors to subscribe.

3. Host Contests or Giveaways

Run contests or giveaways to incentivize visitors to join your email list:

- **Prizes**: Offer enticing prizes such as products, gift cards, or experiences that appeal to your target audience.
- **Entry Requirement**: Require participants to subscribe to your email list as a condition of entry, encouraging them to opt in for a chance to win.
- **Promotion**: Promote your contest or giveaway through various channels, including social media, email, and your website, to maximize visibility and participation.

4. Use Social Media to Promote

Harness the power of social media to expand your email list:

- **Promote Lead Magnets**: Share links to your lead magnets or gated content on social media platforms to attract new subscribers.
- **Host Live Events**: Host live webinars, Q&A sessions, or virtual events and require registration with an email address to participate.
- **Run Social Media Ads**: Launch targeted social media advertising campaigns that drive traffic to dedicated landing pages with sign-up forms.

5. Collaborate with Influencers or Partners

Partner with influencers, brands, or organizations in your niche to reach new audiences and grow your email list:

- **Co-host Webinars or Events**: Collaborate on joint webinars, workshops, or events where participants are required to subscribe to your email list to attend.
- **Cross-Promotion**: Exchange shoutouts, guest blog posts, or social media mentions with partners to promote each other's email lists and reach new subscribers.
- **Affiliate Partnerships**: Offer affiliate partnerships where partners earn commissions or incentives for referring new subscribers to your email list.

6. Provide Exclusive Benefits for Subscribers

Offer exclusive benefits or rewards to subscribers to incentivize sign-ups and encourage retention:

- **Discounts or Promotions**: Provide subscribers with exclusive discounts, promotions, or early access to sales and product launches.
- **Freebies or Samples**: Offer freebies, samples, or bonus content as a thank you for subscribing to your email list.
- **VIP Access**: Grant subscribers VIP access to special events, content, or experiences not available to the general public.

Effective list-building is essential for growing your email list and expanding your audience reach. By implementing strategies such as creating compelling lead magnets, optimizing website sign-up forms, hosting contests or giveaways, leveraging social media, collaborating with influencers or partners, and providing exclusive benefits for subscribers, you can attract engaged subscribers who are interested in your brand and eager to receive your communications. By continuously refining and optimizing your list-building efforts, you can nurture relationships with your audience, drive engagement, and achieve your email marketing goals.

2.3 Opt-In Methods and Signup Forms

Opt-in methods and signup forms play a pivotal role in acquiring subscribers for your email list. By employing effective opt-in strategies and designing user-friendly signup forms, you can attract more subscribers and enhance the overall experience for your audience. In this section, we explore various opt-in methods and best practices for creating signup forms that convert.

1. Single Opt-In vs. Double Opt-In

- **Single Opt-In**: With single opt-in, subscribers only need to enter their email address to join your email list. This method offers simplicity and convenience, making it easy for users to subscribe. However, it may result in higher spam and invalid email addresses.
- **Double Opt-In**: Double opt-in requires subscribers to confirm their subscription by clicking a verification link sent to their email address. While this method adds an extra step to the signup

process, it helps ensure the validity of email addresses and reduces the risk of spam complaints.

2. Types of Opt-In Methods

Website Sign-Up Forms

Embed sign-up forms on your website to capture email addresses from visitors. Place forms strategically on high-traffic pages, such as the homepage, blog posts, or landing pages, and incentivize sign-ups with compelling offers or lead magnets.

Pop-Up or Overlay Forms

Use pop-up or overlay forms to capture visitors' attention and encourage them to subscribe. Customize the timing, frequency, and design of pop-ups to align with user behavior and preferences, and offer incentives or discounts to incentivize sign-ups.

Exit-Intent Pop-Ups

Trigger exit-intent pop-ups when visitors are about to leave your website, offering them a last chance to subscribe before exiting. Use engaging copy and visuals to entice visitors to stay and provide their email addresses in exchange for valuable content or offers.

Embedded Forms in Content

Embed sign-up forms within your content, such as blog posts, articles, or videos, to capture email addresses from engaged readers or viewers. Offer relevant lead magnets or content upgrades that complement the topic of the content and incentivize sign-ups.

Social Media Sign-Up Buttons

Utilize social media platforms to promote your email list and encourage sign-ups. Add sign-up buttons or links to your social media profiles, bios, or posts, directing followers to dedicated landing pages or sign-up forms on your website.

3. Best Practices for Signup Forms

Keep It Simple

Keep signup forms concise and easy to fill out, asking for only essential information such as name and email address. Minimize the number of form fields to reduce friction and increase conversions.

Use Clear and Compelling Headlines

Use clear and compelling headlines that communicate the value proposition and incentivize visitors to subscribe. Highlight the benefits of joining your email list and what subscribers can expect to receive.

Provide Visual Cues

Use visual cues such as arrows, icons, or contrasting colors to draw attention to the sign-up form and guide users' focus toward the call-to-action (CTA) button. Ensure that the CTA button stands out and is easily clickable.

Offer Incentives or Lead Magnets

Offer incentives or lead magnets such as ebooks, guides, or discounts to entice visitors to subscribe to your email list. Communicate the value of the incentive and what subscribers will gain by signing up.

Include Privacy Assurance

Include a privacy assurance statement or link to your privacy policy to reassure visitors that their information will be kept secure and not shared with third parties. Building trust is essential for encouraging sign-ups and maintaining a positive reputation.

By implementing effective opt-in strategies and designing user-friendly signup forms, you can attract more subscribers and enhance the overall experience for your audience. Whether through website sign-up forms, pop-up overlays, embedded forms in content, or social media sign-up buttons, the goal is to make it easy and enticing for visitors to join your email list. By following best practices such as keeping forms simple, using clear headlines, providing visual cues, offering incentives, and ensuring privacy assurance, you can maximize sign-up conversions and grow your email list effectively.

2.4 Ensuring Ethical Practices and Compliance

Maintaining ethical practices and compliance with regulations is paramount in email marketing to protect both your brand reputation and the privacy of your subscribers. By adhering to ethical standards and regulatory requirements, you can build trust with your audience and avoid legal repercussions. In this section, we explore key considerations for ensuring ethical practices and compliance in email marketing.

1. Permission-Based Marketing

Adopt a permission-based approach to email marketing, where subscribers willingly opt-in to receive communications from your brand. Avoid purchasing or renting email lists, as this can lead to spam complaints and damage your sender's reputation. Instead, focus on building your email list organically through opt-in methods such as website sign-up forms, lead magnets, and social media promotions.

2. Compliance with Anti-Spam Laws

Familiarize yourself with anti-spam laws and regulations that govern email marketing practices in your jurisdiction, such as:

- **CAN-SPAM Act (United States)**: Ensure compliance with the CAN-SPAM Act by including accurate sender information, clear subject lines, and a visible unsubscribe mechanism in every marketing email.

- **CASL (Canada)**: Comply with the Canadian Anti-Spam Legislation (CASL) by obtaining express consent from recipients before sending commercial electronic messages (CEMs) and providing a clear opt-out mechanism.
- **GDPR (European Union)**: Adhere to the General Data Protection Regulation (GDPR) by obtaining explicit consent from EU residents before processing their data and providing transparency about data collection, storage, and usage practices.

3. Transparent Data Collection and Usage

Be transparent about your data collection and usage practices to build trust with your subscribers. Communicate how you will use their information, including the types of emails they can expect to receive, the frequency of communication, and how their data will be protected. Provide links to your privacy policy and ensure that subscribers have the option to update their preferences or unsubscribe at any time.

4. Honoring Subscriber Preferences

Respect subscriber preferences and honor their requests promptly. Provide easy-to-find unsubscribe options in every marketing email and ensure that unsubscribe requests are processed promptly and efficiently. Additionally, offers options for subscribers to update their preferences, such as choosing the types of emails they wish to receive or adjusting email frequency.

5. Secure Data Storage and Transmission

Implement robust security measures to protect subscriber data against unauthorized access, breaches, or misuse. Use encryption protocols to secure data transmission and storage, regularly update software and systems to address security vulnerabilities, and restrict access to sensitive information only to authorized personnel.

6. Monitoring and Compliance Audits

Regularly monitor your email marketing practices and conduct compliance audits to ensure adherence to ethical standards and regulatory requirements. Review your email content, subscriber lists, and data handling processes to identify and address any potential issues or violations proactively. Stay informed about updates to relevant laws and regulations and adjust your practices accordingly to maintain compliance.

Ensuring ethical practices and compliance with regulations is essential for maintaining trust with your audience and safeguarding the integrity of your email marketing efforts. By adopting permission-based marketing, complying with anti-spam laws, transparently communicating data collection and usage practices, honoring subscriber preferences, securing data storage and transmission, and conducting regular compliance audits, you can demonstrate your commitment to ethical standards and legal compliance in email marketing. By prioritizing ethical practices and compliance, you can build stronger relationships with your subscribers and mitigate the risks associated with non-compliance.

Chapter 3: Crafting Effective Email Content

Email content serves as the heart of your email marketing strategy, playing a pivotal role in engaging subscribers, driving conversions, and achieving your marketing goals. In this chapter, we delve into the art of crafting effective email content that resonates with your audience, captivates their attention, and inspires action.

1.   Understanding Your Audience

Before diving into content creation, it's crucial to understand your audience - their needs, preferences, challenges, and aspirations. By gaining insights into your audience's demographics, psychographics, and behaviors, you can tailor your email content to address their specific interests and pain points effectively.

2.   Defining Clear Objectives

Define clear objectives for your email campaigns, whether it's driving sales, increasing website traffic, promoting brand awareness, or nurturing customer relationships. Having clear goals in mind will guide your content creation process and ensure that your emails deliver value and relevance to your audience.

3.   Crafting Compelling Subject Lines

Subject lines are the first impression your email makes on subscribers, influencing whether they open or ignore your message. Craft compelling subject lines that are concise, intriguing, and relevant to the content of your email. Use personalization, urgency, curiosity, or benefit-driven language to entice recipients to open your email.

4.   Engaging Introductory Content

Hook your audience from the start with engaging introductory content that grabs their attention and sets the tone for the rest of the email. Use storytelling, compelling statistics, or intriguing questions to captivate readers and draw them into your message.

5.   Providing Value-Driven Content

Deliver value to your subscribers by providing content that addresses their needs, solves their problems, or fulfills their desires. Offer educational resources, helpful tips, industry insights, or exclusive offers that resonate with your audience and demonstrate your expertise and authority in your niche.

6.   Incorporating Visual Elements

Enhance the visual appeal of your emails by incorporating eye-catching images, graphics, videos, or GIFs that complement your written content. Visual elements not only break up text but also capture attention and convey information more engagingly and memorably.

7. Call-to-Action (CTA) Optimization

Optimize your call-to-action (CTA) to encourage desired actions from your subscribers, whether it's making a purchase, signing up for a webinar, or downloading a resource. Use clear, action-oriented language, contrasting colors, and prominent placement to make your CTA stand out and compel recipients to take action.

8. Mobile-Friendly Design

Ensure that your email content is optimized for mobile devices, as a significant portion of your audience is likely to access emails on smartphones or tablets. Use responsive design principles to create emails that adapt seamlessly to different screen sizes and devices, providing a consistent and user-friendly experience across all platforms.

9. Personalization and Segmentation

Personalize your email content based on subscriber preferences, behaviors, and demographics to create more relevant and targeted messages. Segment your email list into distinct groups and tailor your content to each segment's interests, preferences, and purchase history, increasing engagement and conversion rates.

10. Testing and Optimization

Continuously test and optimize your email content to improve performance and achieve better results over time. Experiment with different subject lines, content formats, CTAs, and send times to identify what resonates best with your audience. Analyze key metrics such as open rates, click-through rates, and conversion rates to gauge effectiveness and make data-driven decisions for future campaigns.

Crafting effective email content is both an art and a science, requiring a deep understanding of your audience, clear objectives, and strategic execution. By following best practices such as understanding your audience, defining clear objectives, crafting compelling subject lines, providing value-driven content, incorporating visual elements, optimizing CTAs, designing for mobile, personalizing and segmenting, and testing and optimizing, you can create emails that resonate with your subscribers, drive engagement, and achieve your marketing goals. Embrace creativity, stay informed about industry trends, and always put your audience's needs first to create email content that captivates, inspires, and delivers results.

3.1 Writing Engaging Subject Lines

Subject lines are the gateway to your emails, determining whether recipients will open and engage with your message or consign it to the depths of their inbox. Crafting engaging subject lines is an art form that requires creativity, relevance, and an understanding of your audience's preferences. In this section, we explore strategies for writing subject lines that captivate attention and compel recipients to open your emails.

1. Personalization

Incorporate personalization elements such as the recipient's name or location to make subject lines feel tailored to individual recipients. Personalized subject lines can create a sense of connection and relevance, increasing the likelihood of openness and engagement.

2. Curiosity and Intrigue

Evoke curiosity and intrigue by posing questions, teasing content, or offering a sneak peek of what's inside the email. Subject lines that pique recipients' curiosity compel them to open the email to satisfy their curiosity and discover more.

3. Urgency and Scarcity

Create a sense of urgency or scarcity by using time-sensitive language or indicating limited availability. Phrases like "Last Chance," "Limited Time Offer," or "Act Now" instill a fear of missing out (FOMO) and prompt recipients to take immediate action.

4. Benefit-Driven Language

Focus on the benefits or value proposition of your email content to entice recipients to open and engage. Highlight what recipients stand to gain or learn by opening the email, emphasizing the value they'll receive from reading the content inside.

5. Clarity and Conciseness

Keep subject lines clear, concise, and to the point, avoiding unnecessary words or jargon. A succinct subject line that communicates the essence of the email content at a glance is more likely to capture attention and drive opens.

6. A/B Testing

Experiment with different subject line variations through A/B testing to determine which resonates best with your audience. Test factors such as length, tone, personalization, and urgency to identify the most effective subject line strategies for your email campaigns.

7. Avoiding Spam Triggers

Steer clear of spam triggers such as excessive punctuation, all caps, or overly sales language in your subject lines. Emails that trigger spam filters are less likely to reach recipients' inboxes, undermining your efforts to engage with your audience.

8. Segment-Specific Messaging

Tailor subject lines to specific audience segments based on their interests, preferences, or behaviors. Segment-specific messaging ensures that subject lines are relevant and resonant with each audience segment, driving higher open rates and engagement.

9. Emoji and Symbols

Consider incorporating emojis or symbols sparingly in subject lines to add visual interest and personality. Emojis can help subject lines stand out in crowded inboxes and convey emotion or context more effectively.

10. Test and Iterate

Continuously test and iterate on your subject line strategies to optimize performance over time. Analyze open rates, click-through rates, and conversion rates to gauge the effectiveness of different subject line approaches and refine your tactics accordingly.

Writing engaging subject lines is a critical component of email marketing success, influencing recipients' decision to open or ignore your emails. By incorporating personalization, curiosity, urgency, benefit-driven language, clarity, A/B testing, spam trigger avoidance, segment-specific messaging, emojis, and continuous testing and iteration into your subject line strategies, you can increase open rates, drive engagement, and ultimately, achieve your email marketing goals. Experiment with different tactics, monitor performance metrics and adapt your approach based on audience feedback to craft subject lines that compel recipients to take action.

3.2 Personalizing Email Content

Personalization is a powerful strategy for enhancing the effectiveness of your email marketing campaigns, allowing you to tailor content to the unique preferences, interests, and behaviors of individual recipients. By delivering personalized experiences, you can increase engagement, drive conversions, and foster stronger connections with your audience. In this section, we explore strategies for personalizing email content to maximize relevance and impact.

1. Dynamic Content Insertion

Utilize dynamic content insertion to customize email content based on recipient data such as name, location, past purchases, or browsing history. By dynamically inserting personalized elements into emails, you can create a sense of individualization and relevance that resonates with each recipient.

2. Segmentation and Targeting

Segment your email list into distinct groups based on demographic, behavioral, or psychographic attributes, and tailor content to each segment's specific interests and preferences. By sending targeted emails that address the unique needs of different audience segments, you can increase relevance and engagement.

3. Behavioral Triggers

Implement behavioral triggers that automatically send personalized emails based on recipient actions or interactions with your brand. For example, send a welcome email series to new subscribers, abandoned cart emails to shoppers who leave items in their cart, or re-engagement emails to inactive subscribers.

4. Purchase History Recommendations

Recommend products or services based on recipients' past purchase history or browsing behavior. Use data analysis and machine learning algorithms to identify relevant recommendations that align with each recipient's preferences and purchase patterns.

5. Personalized Subject Lines and Preheaders

Craft personalized subject lines and preheaders that grab recipients' attention and entice them to open the email. Incorporate the recipient's name, past purchase history, or location into subject lines and preheaders to create a sense of individualized communication.

6. Customized Content Blocks

Create customized content blocks within emails that display different content based on recipient characteristics or behaviors. For example, showcase products or offers that are relevant to each recipient's preferences or segment membership.

7.   Lifecycle Stage Messaging

Tailor email content to match recipients' lifecycle stage, whether they're new subscribers, active customers, or lapsed users. Deliver content that addresses their specific needs, challenges, or interests at each stage of the customer journey to drive engagement and retention.

8.   Preference Center Options

Provide recipients with options to customize their email preferences through a preference center. Allow them to choose the types of emails they wish to receive, frequency of communication, and areas of interest, empowering them to personalize their email experience.

9.   Personalized Recommendations and Offers

Deliver personalized recommendations and offers based on recipients' past behavior, preferences, or interactions with your brand. Whether it's tailored product recommendations, exclusive discounts, or personalized content suggestions, personalized offers can drive engagement and conversions.

10. Continuous Testing and Optimization

Continuously test and optimize your personalization strategies to improve performance and relevance over time. Monitor key metrics such as open rates, click-through rates, and conversion rates to gauge the effectiveness of personalized content and refine your approach based on audience feedback.

Personalizing email content allows you to create meaningful and relevant experiences for your audience, driving higher engagement, loyalty, and conversions. By leveraging dynamic content insertion, segmentation, behavioral triggers, purchase history recommendations, personalized subject lines, customized content blocks, lifecycle stage messaging, preference center options, personalized recommendations and offers, and continuous testing and optimization, you can deliver tailored content that resonates with each recipient and fosters stronger connections with your brand. Embrace personalization as a cornerstone of your email marketing strategy, and prioritize delivering value and relevance to your audience at every touchpoint.

3.3 Content Strategies for Different Campaign Types

Different email marketing campaigns serve distinct purposes and require tailored content strategies to achieve their objectives effectively. Whether you're sending promotional emails, newsletters, welcome series, or transactional messages, crafting compelling content that resonates with your audience is essential. In this section, we explore content strategies for various types of email marketing campaigns to maximize engagement and drive results.

1. Promotional Emails

Objective: Drive sales, generate leads, or promote special offers and discounts.

Content Strategy:

- Highlight compelling offers, discounts, or promotions.
- Create a sense of urgency or scarcity to encourage immediate action.
- Showcase product features, benefits, or customer testimonials.
- Include clear and prominent call-to-action (CTA) buttons.
- Personalize content based on recipient preferences or past purchase history.
- Use visually appealing images or graphics to grab attention.

2. Newsletters

Objective: Provide valuable information, updates, or resources to subscribers.

Content Strategy:

- Curate relevant and interesting content from your blog, industry news, or third-party sources.
- Share educational resources, how-to guides, or tips and tricks.
- Include company updates, announcements, or success stories.
- Incorporate visual elements such as images, videos, or infographics.
- Segment newsletters based on subscriber interests or preferences.
- Encourage engagement through polls, surveys, or user-generated content.

3. Welcome Series

Objective: Onboard new subscribers, introduce them to your brand, and nurture relationships.

Content Strategy:

- Send a series of emails that introduce your brand, products, or services.
- Welcome new subscribers and thank them for joining your email list.
- Provide valuable resources or exclusive content to educate and engage.
- Encourage subscribers to connect with your brand on social media or visit your website.
- Personalize content based on subscriber preferences or interests.
- Set expectations for future communication and encourage subscribers to update their preferences.

4. Transactional Emails

Objective: Provide essential information or confirmations related to customer transactions or interactions.

Content Strategy:

- Deliver order confirmations, shipping notifications, or delivery updates.
- Provide receipts, invoices, or payment confirmations.
- Include personalized product recommendations based on past purchases.
- Encourage post-purchase actions such as leaving a review or referring a friend.
- Use clear and concise language to convey information effectively.
- Maintain brand consistency and professionalism in transactional email design and messaging.

5. Re-engagement Campaigns

Objective: Re-engage inactive subscribers and encourage them to re-engage with your brand.

Content Strategy:

- Send personalized emails that acknowledge the recipient's inactivity.
- Offer incentives, discounts, or exclusive offers to entice re-engagement.
- Remind subscribers of the value they'll receive from staying subscribed.
- Prompt subscribers to update their preferences or interests.
- Use compelling subject lines and engaging content to grab attention.

- Provide a clear and easy way for subscribers to opt back in or unsubscribe if desired.

6. Seasonal or Holiday Campaigns

Objective: Capitalize on seasonal events or holidays to promote special offers, discounts, or themed content.

Content Strategy:

- Create themed email content that aligns with the season or holiday.
- Offer exclusive promotions, discounts, or limited-time offers.
- Incorporate seasonal imagery, colors, or graphics to enhance visual appeal.
- Share holiday-themed content, recipes, gift guides, or DIY ideas.
- Personalize content to reflect recipients' preferences or past purchase behavior.
- Use urgency and scarcity to drive action, such as countdowns or limited-time offers.

Tailoring your content strategy to the specific objectives and audience of each email marketing campaign is essential for maximizing engagement and driving results. Whether you're sending promotional emails, newsletters, welcome series, transactional messages, re-engagement campaigns, or seasonal/holiday campaigns, the key is to deliver relevant, valuable, and compelling content that resonates with your audience and encourages action. By understanding the unique characteristics and goals of each campaign type and implementing effective content strategies, you can create impactful email experiences that foster stronger connections with your subscribers and drive success for your brand.

3.4 Visual Design and Layout Best Practices

Visual design and layout play a crucial role in creating engaging and effective email marketing campaigns. A well-designed email not only captures attention but also enhances readability, communicates your brand identity, and drives action. In this section, we explore best practices for visual design and layout to optimize the effectiveness of your email campaigns.

1. Clean and Mobile-Responsive Design

Objective: Ensure your emails display properly and are easy to read across various devices and screen sizes.

Best Practices:

- Use a clean and clutter-free design with ample white space.
- Optimize emails for mobile devices with responsive design principles.
- Test emails on different devices and email clients to ensure compatibility.

2. Consistent Branding

Objective: Reinforce your brand identity and create a cohesive brand experience for subscribers.

Best Practices:

- Use consistent branding elements such as colors, fonts, and logos.
- Incorporate brand visuals and imagery that align with your brand's aesthetic.
- Ensure brand elements are prominently displayed and easily recognizable.

3. Visual Hierarchy

Objective: Guide readers' attention and prioritize content effectively within the email.

Best Practices:

- Use hierarchy to organize content based on importance and relevance.
- Place key information and CTAs prominently at the top of the email.
- Use headings, subheadings, and formatting to differentiate content sections.

4. Compelling Imagery and Graphics

Objective: Capture attention and enhance engagement with visually appealing imagery and graphics.

Best Practices:

- Use high-quality images that are relevant to your message and resonate with your audience.
- Incorporate eye-catching graphics, icons, or illustrations to complement text content.
- Optimize image file sizes for faster loading times without compromising quality.

5. Clear and Readable Text

Objective: Ensure text content is easy to read and digest for recipients.

Best Practices:

- Use legible fonts and font sizes that are easy to read on both desktop and mobile devices.
- Maintain a contrast between text and background colors for readability.
- Limit the use of long paragraphs and break up text with headings, bullet points, and white space.

6. Effective Use of CTAs

Objective: Encourage recipients to take desired actions within the email.

Best Practices:

- Use clear and actionable language for CTAs that communicate the desired action.
- Make CTAs prominent with contrasting colors, larger font sizes, or buttons.
- Place CTAs strategically within the email, such as at the top, middle, and end.

7. Scannable Content

Objective: Make it easy for recipients to quickly scan and digest the email content.

Best Practices:

- Organize content into digestible sections with descriptive headings.
- Highlight important information using bold text, color, or formatting.
- Use bullet points or numbered lists to present information in a concise and structured format.

8. Testing and Optimization

Objective: Continuously improve email design and layout based on performance data and recipient feedback.

Best Practices:

- Conduct A/B testing to compare different design elements, layouts, and CTAs.
- Analyze performance metrics such as open rates, click-through rates, and conversions.
- Solicit feedback from recipients through surveys or feedback forms to identify areas for improvement.

Visual design and layout are essential components of successful email marketing campaigns, influencing recipients' perception and engagement with your content. By following best practices such as clean and mobile-responsive design, consistent branding, visual hierarchy, compelling imagery, clear and readable text, effective use of CTAs, scannable content, and testing and optimization, you can create emails that capture attention, drive action, and deliver results. Invest time and resources into crafting visually appealing and user-friendly emails that align with your brand identity and resonate with your audience, ultimately leading to improved engagement and conversions for your business.

Chapter 4: Designing and Sending Emails

Designing and sending emails is a critical aspect of email marketing that requires careful planning, creativity, and attention to detail. From creating visually appealing designs to optimizing deliverability and tracking performance, every step in the email design and sending process contributes to the success of your campaigns. In this chapter, we explore best practices and strategies for designing and sending emails that engage subscribers, drive conversions, and achieve your marketing goals.

1. Planning Your Email Campaign

Before diving into the design and sending process, it's essential to plan your email campaign strategically. Consider the following factors:

- **Campaign Objectives**: Define clear goals for your email campaign, whether it's driving sales, increasing website traffic, promoting brand awareness, or nurturing customer relationships.
- **Target Audience**: Identify your target audience and segment your email list based on demographics, behaviors, or interests to ensure relevant messaging.
- **Content Strategy**: Determine the type of content you'll include in your emails, such as promotional offers, educational resources, or company updates.
- **Cadence and Timing**: Decide on the frequency and timing of your email sends to maximize engagement without overwhelming subscribers.

- **Automation Opportunities**: Explore opportunities for automation, such as welcome series, abandoned cart emails, or drip campaigns, to streamline your email marketing efforts.

2. Designing Compelling Email Templates

Creating visually appealing and user-friendly email templates is essential for capturing subscribers' attention and delivering your message effectively. Consider the following design principles:

- **Mobile Responsiveness**: Ensure your email templates are optimized for mobile devices, with a responsive design that adapts to different screen sizes.
- **Branding Consistency**: Maintain consistent branding elements such as colors, fonts, and logos across all email templates to reinforce brand identity.
- **Clear Call-to-Action (CTA)**: Place prominent and actionable CTAs within your email templates to encourage recipients to take desired actions.
- **Visual Hierarchy**: Organize content using visual hierarchy principles to guide readers' attention and prioritize important information.
- **Whitespace and Clutter-Free Design**: Use whitespace effectively to create breathing room and avoid clutter, ensuring a clean and easy-to-read layout.

3. Crafting Engaging Email Content

Compelling email content is essential for capturing subscribers' interest and driving engagement. Follow these tips for crafting engaging email content:

- **Personalization**: Personalize email content based on recipient data such as name, location, or past purchase history to create a sense of individualization.
- **Relevant and Valuable Information**: Provide content that is relevant and valuable to your audience, whether it's product recommendations, industry insights, or exclusive offers.
- **Clear and Concise Messaging**: Keep email content concise and to the point, with clear messaging that communicates the intended purpose effectively.
- **Visual Elements**: Incorporate eye-catching visuals such as images, videos, or GIFs to enhance the visual appeal of your emails and communicate information more effectively.

4. Optimizing Deliverability and Compliance

Ensuring that your emails reach recipients' inboxes and comply with relevant regulations is crucial for the success of your email campaigns. Consider the following best practices:

- **Email Authentication**: Implement email authentication protocols such as SPF, DKIM, and DMARC to verify the authenticity of your emails and prevent spoofing or phishing attacks.

- **List Hygiene**: Regularly clean and maintain your email list by removing inactive or invalid email addresses to improve deliverability and sender reputation.
- **Compliance with Anti-Spam Laws**: Familiarize yourself with anti-spam laws such as CAN-SPAM, GDPR, and CASL, and ensure that your email campaigns comply with relevant regulations.
- **Opt-Out Mechanism**: Include a clear and visible opt-out mechanism in every email to allow recipients to unsubscribe easily and comply with anti-spam regulations.

5. Testing and Optimization

Testing and optimization are essential for identifying areas for improvement and maximizing the effectiveness of your email campaigns. Consider the following strategies:

- **A/B Testing**: Conduct A/B tests on different elements of your emails, such as subject lines, CTAs, or content, to determine what resonates best with your audience.
- **Segmentation Testing**: Test different segmentation strategies to identify the most effective ways to target and personalize your email campaigns.
- **Delivery Timing**: Experiment with different send times and days of the week to determine when your emails are most likely to be opened and engaged with.
- **Performance Tracking**: Monitor key performance metrics such as open rates, click-through rates, and conversion rates to gauge the

effectiveness of your email campaigns and identify areas for improvement.

Designing and sending emails is a multifaceted process that requires careful planning, creativity, and optimization. By following best practices for planning your email campaign, designing compelling email templates, crafting engaging content, optimizing deliverability and compliance, and testing and optimization, you can create email campaigns that capture subscribers' attention, drive engagement, and achieve your marketing objectives. Embrace experimentation, monitor performance metrics, and continuously refine your approach to email marketing to maximize results and deliver value to your audience.

4.1 Creating Responsive Email Templates

In today's digital landscape, where a significant portion of email opens occurs on mobile devices, creating responsive email templates is essential for ensuring optimal user experience and engagement. Responsive design ensures that your emails display correctly and are easy to read across various devices and screen sizes, including smartphones, tablets, and desktops. Follow these best practices to create responsive email templates:

1. **Use a Mobile-First Approach**

Start by designing your email template with mobile devices in mind. Since mobile screens have limited space, prioritize the most important content and ensure it is easily accessible and legible on smaller screens.

2. Utilize Fluid Layouts

Design your email template using fluid layouts that adapt and scale proportionally to different screen sizes. Avoid fixed-width designs, as they may not display properly on mobile devices with varying screen dimensions.

3. Optimize Font Sizes and Line Heights

Choose font sizes and line heights that are legible on both small and large screens. Use relative font sizes (e.g., percentages or ems) rather than absolute pixel values to ensure consistency across devices.

4. Simplify Navigation and Interaction

Streamline navigation and interaction elements such as buttons and links to accommodate touch-based interactions on mobile devices. Ensure that clickable elements are large enough to be tapped easily without accidental clicks.

5. Minimize Image File Sizes

Optimize images to reduce file sizes and improve loading times, especially on mobile networks. Use image compression techniques and consider using CSS for simple graphics and icons whenever possible to minimize reliance on images.

6. Test Across Multiple Devices and Email Clients

Test your responsive email templates across various devices, email clients, and screen sizes to ensure consistent rendering and functionality. Use testing tools and services to identify and address any compatibility issues.

7. Include Media Query Breakpoints

Incorporate media query breakpoints into your CSS to define specific styles for different screen sizes. Use breakpoints to adjust layout, font sizes, and other design elements based on the device's screen width.

8. Optimize for Touch Gestures

Design email templates with touch-friendly elements and spacing to accommodate mobile users' gestures such as swiping and tapping. Ensure that links and buttons are sufficiently spaced apart to prevent accidental clicks.

9. Test Interactivity and Animation

If incorporating interactivity or animation into your email templates, ensure compatibility with popular email clients and mobile devices. Test interactive elements such as accordions, carousels, and hamburger menus across various platforms.

10. Stay Up-to-Date with Best Practices

Keep abreast of evolving best practices and trends in responsive email design to adapt your templates accordingly. Regularly review and update your templates to ensure they remain effective and compatible with the latest devices and email clients.

Creating responsive email templates is essential for delivering a consistent and engaging user experience across devices and maximizing the impact of your email marketing campaigns. By following best practices such as adopting a mobile-first approach, utilizing fluid layouts, optimizing font sizes and line heights, simplifying navigation, minimizing image file sizes, testing across multiple devices, including media query breakpoints, optimizing for touch gestures, testing interactivity and animation, and staying up-to-date with best practices, you can ensure that your emails are well-received and effective at engaging your audience, regardless of the device they use.

4.2 Importance of Mobile Optimization

In today's digital landscape, mobile optimization is not just a nice-to-have; it's a necessity for successful email marketing campaigns. With the proliferation of smartphones and the increasing preference for mobile browsing, ensuring that your emails are optimized for mobile devices is critical for engaging subscribers, driving conversions, and maximizing the effectiveness of your email marketing efforts. Here's why mobile optimization is so important:

1. Mobile Device Usage is Pervasive

The majority of email opens now occur on mobile devices, surpassing desktop opens in many industries. With people constantly on the go and relying on their smartphones for communication and information, it's essential to deliver a seamless and enjoyable experience for mobile users.

2. Improved User Experience

Mobile-optimized emails provide a better user experience for recipients by ensuring that content is displayed correctly and is easy to read and interact with on small screens. A positive user experience increases engagement, encourages further interaction with your brand, and fosters customer loyalty.

3. Higher Open and Click-Through Rates

Mobile-optimized emails tend to have higher open and click-through rates compared to non-optimized emails. By catering to the preferences and behaviors of mobile users, you can capture their attention more effectively and compel them to take action, whether it's making a purchase, visiting your website, or engaging with your content.

4. Positive Brand Perception

Delivering well-designed and functional emails on mobile devices reflects positively on your brand image. It demonstrates that you value the convenience and preferences of your audience and are committed to providing a top-notch user experience across all touchpoints.

5. Maximizing Reach and Engagement

Mobile optimization ensures that your emails reach the widest possible audience and are accessible to users regardless of the device they use. By reaching users where they are most active and engaged, you can maximize the impact of your email campaigns and drive meaningful results for your business.

6. Adaptation to Changing Consumer Behavior

As consumer behavior continues to evolve, businesses must adapt to meet the changing preferences and expectations of their audience. Mobile optimization is not just a trend; it's a reflection of how people prefer to consume content and interact with brands in today's mobile-centric world.

7. Competitive Advantage

In a competitive marketplace, mobile optimization can give you a significant edge over competitors who have yet to prioritize mobile-friendly email design. By delivering superior user experiences and engaging mobile content, you can stand out from the crowd and capture the attention of mobile-savvy consumers.

Mobile optimization is no longer optional for email marketers; it's a fundamental requirement for success in today's digital landscape. By prioritizing mobile-friendly design, ensuring seamless user experiences, and catering to the preferences of mobile users, you can enhance engagement, drive conversions, and stay ahead of the competition. Embrace mobile optimization as a cornerstone of your email marketing strategy and reap the rewards of reaching and engaging with your audience wherever they are.

4.3 Scheduling and Frequency of Email Sends

Determining the optimal scheduling and frequency of email sends is crucial for maintaining subscriber engagement, maximizing open rates, and achieving your email marketing goals. Finding the right balance between staying top-of-mind and avoiding inbox overload requires careful consideration of your audience's preferences, behaviors, and the nature of your email content. Here's how to approach scheduling and frequency effectively:

1. Understand Your Audience

Start by understanding your audience's preferences, habits, and time zones. Analyze past email performance data to identify patterns in open rates, click-through rates, and engagement metrics. Consider conducting surveys or gathering feedback to learn more about when and how often subscribers prefer to receive emails.

2. Segment Your Email List

Segment your email list based on factors such as demographics, purchase history, engagement level, and preferences. Different segments may have varying preferences regarding email frequency and timing. Tailor your email and send the schedule to each segment's unique characteristics and needs to ensure relevance and maximize engagement.

3. Test Different Send Times

Experiment with different send times and days of the week to determine when your emails are most likely to be opened and engaged with. Conduct A/B tests to compare performance metrics across various send times and identify the optimal timing for your audience. Consider factors such as work schedules, commuting times, and leisure activities when scheduling sends.

4. Consider the Type of Email Campaign

The type of email campaign you're sending may influence the ideal scheduling and frequency. For example:

- **Promotional Emails**: Consider sending promotional emails during peak shopping times, weekends, or holidays when recipients are more likely to be receptive to offers.

- **Newsletters**: Send newsletters at regular intervals, such as weekly or monthly, to provide consistent updates and valuable content to subscribers.
- **Transactional Emails**: Send transactional emails promptly after specific actions or events, such as order confirmations, shipping notifications, or account updates.

5. Balance Frequency with Value

Strive to strike a balance between email frequency and the value you provide to subscribers. Avoid bombarding subscribers with excessive emails that offer little value, as this can lead to fatigue and increased unsubscribe rates. Instead, focus on delivering high-quality content that meets subscribers' needs and interests, even if it means sending emails less frequently.

6. Monitor Engagement Metrics

Regularly monitor key engagement metrics such as open rates, click-through rates, unsubscribe rates, and spam complaints to gauge the effectiveness of your email send schedule and frequency. Adjust your approach based on performance data and subscriber feedback to optimize engagement and retention.

7. Respect Subscriber Preferences

Respect subscribers' preferences and allow them to control their email frequency and preferences through preference centers or subscription management options. Give subscribers the flexibility to choose how often they receive emails and the types of content they're interested in to reduce opt-outs and improve satisfaction.

8. Continuously Iterate and Improve

Email send scheduling and frequency is not a set-it-and-forget-it task; it requires ongoing monitoring, analysis, and optimization. Continuously iterate on your email send strategy based on performance data, industry trends, and subscriber feedback to ensure relevance, engagement, and long-term success.

Finding the right balance in scheduling and frequency of email sends is essential for maintaining subscriber engagement, driving conversions, and achieving your email marketing objectives. By understanding your audience, segmenting your email list, testing different send times, considering the type of email campaign, balancing frequency with value, monitoring engagement metrics, respecting subscriber preferences, and continuously iterating and improving, you can develop an effective email send strategy that resonates with your audience and delivers results for your business. Embrace flexibility, experimentation, and data-driven insights to optimize your email send schedule and frequency over time.

4.4 Tools and Software for Email Marketing

Email marketing tools and software play a crucial role in streamlining the email creation, delivery, and tracking processes, empowering marketers to create engaging campaigns, reach their target audience, and measure performance effectively. With a wide range of tools available, choosing the right ones for your needs can significantly impact the success of your email marketing efforts. Here are some essential tools and software options for email marketing:

1. Email Service Providers (ESPs)

Email service providers offer comprehensive platforms for managing all aspects of email marketing campaigns, including email creation, list management, automation, segmentation, and analytics. Popular ESPs include:

- **Mailchimp**: A user-friendly platform offering customizable templates, automation features, audience segmentation, and robust analytics.
- **Constant Contact**: Known for its drag-and-drop email builder, event management tools, and integrations with e-commerce platforms.
- **Campaign Monitor**: Offers customizable templates, dynamic content, automation workflows, and detailed reporting for data-driven insights.

2. Marketing Automation Platforms

Marketing automation platforms allow marketers to automate repetitive tasks, nurture leads, and deliver personalized experiences across multiple channels, including email. Key players in this space include:

- **HubSpot**: Offers a suite of marketing automation tools, including email marketing, lead nurturing, CRM integration, and advanced analytics.
- **Pardot**: Salesforce's marketing automation solution, offering email marketing, lead scoring, drip campaigns, and ROI reporting for B2B marketers.
- **Marketo**: Known for its robust automation capabilities, lead management features, and integration with Salesforce CRM.

3. Email Design and Testing Tools

Email design and testing tools help marketers create visually appealing and responsive email campaigns while ensuring compatibility across various devices and email clients. Popular options include:

- **Litmus**: Allows marketers to preview and test emails across 90+ email clients and devices, diagnose rendering issues and optimize email design for better performance.
- **Email on Acid**: Offers email testing and optimization tools, spam testing, and accessibility checks to ensure emails are delivered and displayed correctly.

4. Email Tracking and Analytics Software

Email tracking and analytics software provide insights into email performance metrics, allowing marketers to measure the effectiveness of their campaigns and make data-driven decisions. Key solutions include:

- **Google Analytics**: Integrates with email marketing platforms to track website traffic, conversions, and user behavior triggered by email campaigns.
- **Campaign Monitor Insights**: Offers real-time reporting, A/B testing, and engagement analytics to track opens, clicks, conversions, and subscriber behavior.

5. CRM and Email Integration Tools

CRM and email integration tools allow marketers to synchronize customer data between their CRM system and email marketing platform, enabling personalized messaging and segmentation. Notable options include:

- **Salesforce Integration**: Integrates Salesforce CRM with email marketing platforms to sync contacts, track engagement, and automate email workflows based on CRM data.
- **HubSpot CRM**: Seamlessly integrates with HubSpot's email marketing tools, allowing marketers to track email interactions, segment contacts, and personalize campaigns based on CRM data.

6. Email Deliverability Tools

Email deliverability tools help marketers optimize their email deliverability rates and maintain a positive sender reputation by monitoring email-sending practices, identifying potential issues, and providing actionable insights. Examples include:

- **SendGrid**: Offers email deliverability services, sender authentication, and reputation monitoring to ensure high inbox placement rates and deliverability success.
- **Return Path**: Provides email deliverability solutions, inbox placement testing, and sender reputation monitoring to help marketers improve email deliverability and campaign performance.

Selecting the right tools and software for email marketing is essential for maximizing efficiency, effectiveness, and ROI. Whether you're looking for an email service provider, marketing automation platform, design and testing tools, tracking and analytics software, CRM integration solutions, or email deliverability tools, there are plenty of options available to suit your needs and budget. Evaluate your requirements, consider factors such as ease of use, scalability, integration capabilities, and customer support, and choose the tools that best align with your goals and objectives. With the right tools in place, you can streamline your email marketing processes, deliver compelling campaigns, and drive results for your business.

Chapter 5: Segmentation and Automation

Segmentation and automation are two powerful strategies that can significantly enhance the effectiveness and efficiency of your email marketing campaigns. By segmenting your audience based on specific criteria and automating targeted messages and workflows, you can deliver more relevant content, nurture leads, and drive conversions. In this chapter, we delve into the importance of segmentation and automation in email marketing and explore best practices for implementing these strategies effectively.

1. Importance of Segmentation

Segmentation involves dividing your email list into smaller, targeted groups based on specific characteristics, behaviors, or preferences. Here's why segmentation is essential for email marketing success:

- **Relevance**: Segmented emails are more relevant to recipients' interests, leading to higher engagement and conversion rates.
- **Personalization**: Segmentation allows you to personalize email content and messaging based on each segment's unique needs and preferences.
- **Improved Deliverability**: Sending targeted emails to smaller, more engaged segments can improve deliverability rates and reduce the likelihood of emails being marked as spam.
- **Better Insights**: Segmentation provides valuable insights into audience behavior, allowing you to understand what resonates with different segments and refine your email marketing strategy accordingly.

2. Types of Segmentation

There are various ways to segment your email list to create targeted campaigns. Some common segmentation criteria include:

- **Demographic Segmentation**: Divide your audience based on demographic factors such as age, gender, location, or income level.
- **Behavioral Segmentation**: Segment subscribers based on their past interactions with your emails, website, or products, such as purchase history, browsing behavior, or engagement level.
- **Psychographic Segmentation**: Segment based on lifestyle, interests, values, or personality traits to tailor messaging and content to specific audience segments.
- **Firmographic Segmentation**: Relevant for B2B marketers, this involves segmenting based on company size, industry, revenue, or job title.

3. Benefits of Automation

Automation involves using technology to automate repetitive tasks, workflows, and communication processes. Here's why automation is valuable for email marketing:

- **Time and Resource Efficiency**: Automation saves time and resources by streamlining processes, allowing marketers to focus on strategy and creative tasks.

- **Consistency**: Automation ensures consistent messaging and timing across all touchpoints, maintaining brand consistency and reliability.
- **Scalability**: Automation allows you to scale your email marketing efforts efficiently, regardless of the size of your audience or team.
- **Personalization at Scale**: Automation enables personalized communication at scale, delivering targeted messages and content based on subscriber behavior and preferences.

4. Types of Automated Email Campaigns

There are various types of automated email campaigns that you can set up to engage subscribers throughout their customer journey:

- **Welcome Emails**: Sent to new subscribers to introduce them to your brand, set expectations, and encourage engagement.
- **Abandoned Cart Emails**: Remind customers who have abandoned their shopping carts to complete their purchases, potentially recovering lost sales.
- **Drip Campaigns**: Send a series of automated emails over time to nurture leads, educate subscribers, or promote specific products or services.
- **Birthday or Anniversary Emails**: Personalized messages sent on subscribers' birthdays or anniversaries to show appreciation and encourage loyalty.

5. Best Practices for Segmentation and Automation

To maximize the effectiveness of segmentation and automation in your email marketing efforts, consider the following best practices:

- **Start Simple**: Begin with basic segmentation and automation strategies, then gradually refine and expand as you gather more data and insights.
- **Use Data Wisely**: Collect and analyze data effectively to inform your segmentation and automation decisions, ensuring relevance and accuracy.
- **Test and Iterate**: Continuously test different segmentation criteria, messaging, and automation workflows to optimize performance and engagement.
- **Monitor and Measure**: Track key performance metrics such as open rates, click-through rates, conversion rates, and unsubscribe rates to evaluate the effectiveness of your segmentation and automation efforts.

Segmentation and automation are essential components of a successful email marketing strategy, allowing you to deliver personalized, targeted messages at scale. By segmenting your audience based on specific criteria and automating relevant communication workflows, you can increase engagement, drive conversions, and nurture customer relationships more effectively. Embrace segmentation and automation as powerful tools to enhance the efficiency and impact of your email marketing campaigns, ultimately leading to improved results and ROI for your business.

5.1 Benefits of Segmentation

Segmentation is a fundamental strategy in email marketing that offers numerous benefits for marketers seeking to optimize their campaigns and engage their audience effectively. Here are some key benefits of segmentation:

- **Relevance**: Segmentation allows you to tailor your email content and messaging to specific segments of your audience, ensuring that recipients receive information that is relevant to their interests, preferences, and needs. By sending targeted messages, you increase the likelihood of capturing attention and driving engagement.
- **Personalization**: Segmented emails enable you to personalize the user experience for each recipient, making them feel valued and understood. Personalization goes beyond simply addressing recipients by name; it involves delivering content and offers that resonate with their unique characteristics, behaviors, and interactions with your brand.
- **Higher Engagement Rates**: When emails are tailored to the interests and preferences of recipients, they are more likely to capture attention and generate engagement. Segmented campaigns often yield higher open rates, click-through rates, and conversion rates compared to non-segmented campaigns, as they speak directly to the individual needs and motivations of each segment.
- **Improved Deliverability**: Sending targeted emails to smaller, more engaged segments can improve deliverability rates and inbox placement. By focusing on delivering valuable content to recipients who are most likely to engage with it, you reduce the risk of emails being marked as spam or ignored by recipients.

- **Enhanced Customer Experience**: Segmentation allows you to deliver a more personalized and relevant experience throughout the customer journey, from initial interaction to post-purchase communication. By understanding and addressing the unique needs of different segments, you can create a positive and memorable experience that fosters loyalty and advocacy.
- **Optimized Resource Allocation**: By focusing your resources on segments that are most likely to convert or require special attention, you can allocate your time, budget, and efforts more efficiently. Segmentation helps you prioritize opportunities and tailor your marketing strategies to maximize ROI and achieve your business objectives.
- **Insightful Data Analysis**: Segmenting your audience provides valuable insights into their behaviors, preferences, and interactions with your brand. By analyzing data from segmented campaigns, you can gain a deeper understanding of what resonates with different segments and refine your marketing strategies accordingly.
- **Flexibility and Adaptability**: Segmentation allows you to adapt your messaging and offers based on changes in market conditions, customer preferences, or business objectives. By segmenting your audience dynamically and adjusting your campaigns in real-time, you can remain agile and responsive to evolving needs and trends.

In conclusion, segmentation offers a range of benefits that are essential for driving success in email marketing campaigns. By delivering personalized, relevant content to targeted segments of your audience, you can increase engagement, improve deliverability, enhance the customer experience, and achieve your marketing goals more effectively.

5.2 Techniques for Effective Targeting

Effective targeting is essential for maximizing the impact of your email marketing campaigns and engaging your audience in meaningful ways. By understanding your audience's needs, preferences, and behaviors, you can tailor your messaging and offers to resonate with specific segments of your audience. Here are some techniques for effective targeting in email marketing:

- **Demographic Targeting**: Divide your audience based on demographic factors such as age, gender, location, income level, or occupation. Demographic targeting allows you to create tailored messages that appeal to the unique characteristics of each segment.
- **Behavioral Targeting**: Segment your audience based on their past interactions with your emails, website, or products. Behavioral targeting takes into account factors such as purchase history, browsing behavior, engagement level, or response to previous campaigns. By targeting users based on their behavior, you can deliver more relevant and timely messages that address their specific interests and preferences.
- **Psychographic Targeting**: Segment your audience based on psychographic factors such as lifestyle, interests, values, personality traits, or attitudes. Psychographic targeting allows you to create messages that resonate with the emotional and psychological needs of your audience, fostering a deeper connection and engagement.
- **Lifecycle Stage Targeting**: Tailor your messaging and offers based on where subscribers are in the customer lifecycle, such as new leads, active customers, lapsed customers, or advocates. Lifecycle stage targeting allows you to deliver the right message at

the right time, nurturing leads, re-engaging inactive subscribers, and rewarding loyal customers.

- **Preference-Based Targeting**: Allow subscribers to self-segment based on their preferences, interests, or communication frequency preferences. Preference-based targeting empowers subscribers to control their email experience, ensuring that they receive content that is relevant and valuable to them.

- **Predictive Targeting**: Use predictive analytics and machine learning algorithms to anticipate user behavior and preferences based on historical data and patterns. Predictive targeting allows you to identify high-value segments, personalize recommendations, and deliver targeted messages that drive conversion and retention.

- **Dynamic Content Targeting**: Customize email content and offers dynamically based on recipient attributes, behaviors, or preferences. Dynamic content targeting allows you to create personalized experiences for each recipient, increasing relevance and engagement.

- **Segmentation Combinations**: Combine multiple targeting techniques to create highly specific and relevant segments. For example, you can create segments based on a combination of demographic, behavioral, and psychographic factors to target users with precision and effectiveness.

In conclusion, effective targeting is essential for delivering personalized, relevant, and engaging email experiences to your audience. By leveraging a combination of demographic, behavioral, psychographic, lifecycle stage, preference-based, predictive, dynamic content, and segmentation combination techniques, you can tailor your messaging and offers to resonate with specific segments of your audience, driving engagement, conversion, and loyalty.

5.3 Introduction to Email Automation

Email automation is a powerful strategy that allows marketers to streamline and optimize their email marketing efforts by automating repetitive tasks, workflows, and communication processes. With email automation, marketers can deliver timely, relevant messages to subscribers based on their behaviors, preferences, and interactions with the brand. Here's an introduction to email automation and its key components:

1. Automated Workflows

Email automation revolves around the concept of automated workflows, which are predefined sequences of emails triggered by specific actions or events. These workflows allow marketers to send targeted messages to subscribers at the right time, based on their behavior or lifecycle stage. Common automated workflows include welcome series, abandoned cart reminders, post-purchase follow-ups, and re-engagement campaigns.

2. Trigger Events

Trigger events are the actions or events that initiate automated email workflows. These trigger events can include actions such as signing up for a newsletter, making a purchase, abandoning a shopping cart, visiting a specific page on the website, or celebrating a milestone (e.g., a birthday or anniversary). By defining trigger events, marketers can ensure that emails are sent in response to relevant subscriber actions, increasing the likelihood of engagement and conversion.

3. Personalization and Segmentation

Email automation allows for personalized and segmented communication with subscribers, ensuring that each message resonates with its intended audience. Marketers can leverage subscriber data to personalize email content, subject lines, and offers, creating a more relevant and engaging experience for recipients. Segmentation enables marketers to divide their audience into distinct groups based on specific criteria, such as demographics, behaviors, or preferences, and deliver targeted messages tailored to each segment's needs and interests.

4. Drip Campaigns

Drip campaigns are a common type of automated email workflow that involves sending a series of pre-scheduled emails to subscribers over time. These emails are typically spaced out at regular intervals and are designed to nurture leads, educate subscribers, or promote specific products or services. Drip campaigns allow marketers to stay top-of-mind with subscribers, deliver valuable content over time, and guide them through the customer journey.

5. Testing and Optimization

Email automation provides opportunities for testing and optimization to improve campaign performance and effectiveness continually. Marketers can A/B test different elements of automated emails, such as subject lines, content, CTAs and send times, to identify what resonates best with their audience and drives the desired outcomes. By monitoring key performance metrics and iterating on their automated workflows, marketers can refine their strategies over time and maximize the impact of their email marketing efforts.

6. Integration with Other Marketing Channels

Email automation can be integrated seamlessly with other marketing channels and tools, such as CRM systems, social media platforms, and e-commerce platforms. Integration allows for a holistic approach to marketing automation, enabling marketers to leverage data and insights from multiple sources to create more personalized and coordinated campaigns across channels. By syncing customer data and communication efforts across channels, marketers can deliver a cohesive and seamless experience for their audience, driving engagement and conversion across the customer journey.

In conclusion, email automation is a powerful strategy that enables marketers to deliver timely, relevant, and personalized messages to subscribers, streamline their email marketing processes, and drive engagement and conversion. By leveraging automated workflows, trigger events, personalization and segmentation, drip campaigns, testing and optimization, and integration with other marketing channels, marketers can create more effective and efficient email marketing campaigns that resonate with their audience and achieve their business objectives.

5.4 Setting Up Automated Email Workflows

Setting up automated email workflows involves designing and implementing predefined sequences of emails that are triggered by specific actions or events. These workflows enable marketers to deliver timely, relevant messages to subscribers based on their behaviors, preferences, and interactions with the brand. Here's a step-by-step guide to setting up automated email workflows effectively:

1. Define Your Goals and Objectives

Before creating automated email workflows, clearly define your goals and objectives for each workflow. Determine what action or outcome you want to achieve with each workflow, whether it's welcoming new subscribers, nurturing leads, re-engaging inactive subscribers, or promoting specific products or services.

2. Identify Trigger Events

Identify the trigger events that will initiate each automated email workflow. Trigger events can include actions such as signing up for a newsletter, making a purchase, abandoning a shopping cart, downloading a resource, or celebrating a milestone (e.g., a birthday or anniversary). Choose trigger events that are relevant to your goals and align with your subscribers' behaviors and lifecycle stages.

3. Map Out Your Workflow

Map out the sequence of emails that will comprise each automated workflow. Determine the number of emails in the sequence, the content and messaging of each email, the timing and frequency of sends, and any conditional branching based on subscriber actions or behaviors. Consider the subscriber's journey and how you can guide them through the desired outcome or conversion.

4. Create Compelling Email Content

Create compelling email content that aligns with the goals of each workflow and resonates with your target audience. Craft engaging subject lines, personalized messaging, and relevant offers that encourage recipients to take the desired action. Tailor the content of each email to the specific stage of the subscriber's journey and the context of the trigger event.

5. Set Up Automation Rules

Set up automation rules within your email marketing platform to trigger the automated workflows based on the defined trigger events. Configure the rules to detect when a subscriber meets the criteria for a trigger event and automatically initiate the corresponding workflow. Ensure that the automation rules are correctly configured to capture relevant subscriber actions and events accurately.

6. Test and Optimize

Before launching your automated workflows, thoroughly test each workflow to ensure that emails are triggered correctly, content is displayed properly, and links are functioning as intended. Use A/B testing to experiment with different elements of your emails, such as subject lines, content, CTAs, and send times, to identify what resonates best with your audience. Monitor key performance metrics, such as open rates, click-through rates, conversion rates, and unsubscribe rates, and iterate on your workflows based on insights gathered from testing.

7. Launch and Monitor Performance

Once you're satisfied with your automated email workflows, launch them to your subscriber base and monitor their performance closely. Track key performance metrics to assess the effectiveness of each workflow in achieving its goals and objectives. Continuously monitor and analyze performance data, and make adjustments to your workflows as needed to optimize engagement, conversion, and overall success.

8. Iterate and Improve

Email automation is an iterative process that requires ongoing monitoring, analysis, and optimization. Continuously iterate on your automated workflows based on performance data, subscriber feedback, and changes in market conditions or audience preferences. Regularly review and update your workflows to ensure they remain effective, relevant, and aligned with your evolving goals and objectives.

By following these steps, you can effectively set up automated email workflows that engage your audience, drive conversions, and achieve your marketing objectives. With careful planning, thoughtful execution, and continuous optimization, automated email workflows can become powerful tools for nurturing customer relationships and driving business growth.

Chapter 6: Measuring and Analyzing Performance

Measuring and analyzing the performance of your email marketing campaigns is essential for understanding their effectiveness, identifying areas for improvement, and maximizing your return on investment (ROI). In this chapter, we explore the key metrics and techniques for measuring and analyzing email marketing performance effectively.

1. Key Metrics for Email Marketing Performance

- **Open Rate**: The percentage of recipients who open your email out of the total number of emails delivered. The open rate indicates how well your subject lines and sender name resonate with your audience.
- **Click-Through Rate (CTR)**: The percentage of recipients who click on a link or call-to-action (CTA) within your email. CTR measures the effectiveness of your email content and encourages engagement with your website or landing page.
- **Conversion Rate**: The percentage of recipients who complete a desired action, such as making a purchase, filling out a form, or downloading a resource, after clicking on a link in your email. Conversion rate indicates the effectiveness of your email in driving desired outcomes.
- **Bounce Rate**: The percentage of emails that were not successfully delivered to recipients' inboxes due to factors such as invalid email addresses or technical issues. Bounce rate measures the quality of your email list and the deliverability of your emails.
- **Unsubscribe Rate**: The percentage of recipients who opt out of receiving further emails from your mailing list after receiving a

particular email. The unsubscribe rate indicates the level of dissatisfaction or disengagement among your subscribers.

- **List Growth Rate**: The rate at which your email list is growing over time. The list growth rate reflects your ability to attract new subscribers and maintain a healthy email list size.
- **Engagement Rate**: A composite metric that combines open rate, click-through rate, and other engagement metrics to measure overall subscriber engagement with your emails. Engagement rate provides a holistic view of how well your emails are performing.

2. Techniques for Analyzing Performance

- **Segmentation Analysis**: Analyze email performance metrics by segment to identify patterns and trends among different audience groups. Segmenting your data by factors such as demographics, behaviors, or lifecycle stages allows you to tailor your messaging and offers more effectively.
- **A/B Testing**: Conduct A/B tests to compare different elements of your emails, such as subject lines, content, CTAs, send times or design variations. A/B testing helps you identify what resonates best with your audience and optimize your email campaigns for maximum impact.
- **Lifecycle Analysis**: Track the performance of your emails throughout the customer lifecycle, from acquisition to conversion to retention. Analyzing email performance at each stage of the customer journey allows you to tailor your messaging and strategies to the specific needs and behaviors of your audience.
- **Engagement Analysis**: Monitor engagement metrics over time to identify trends and patterns in subscriber behavior. Analyze changes in open rates, click-through rates, and other engagement

metrics to understand how your audience is responding to your emails and adjust your strategies accordingly.

- **ROI Analysis**: Calculate the return on investment (ROI) of your email marketing campaigns by comparing the revenue generated from email conversions to the costs associated with email marketing, such as email platform fees, content creation costs, and staff time. ROI analysis helps you assess the financial performance and effectiveness of your email marketing efforts.
- **Competitive Analysis**: Benchmark your email performance against competitors or industry benchmarks to gain insights into your relative performance and identify areas where you can improve. Analyze factors such as average open rates, click-through rates, and conversion rates to understand how you stack up against the competition.

3. Tools for Measuring and Analyzing Performance

- **Email Analytics Platforms**: Use email analytics platforms such as Google Analytics, Adobe Analytics, or specialized email marketing platforms to track and measure key performance metrics across your email campaigns.
- **A/B Testing Tools**: Utilize A/B testing tools provided by email marketing platforms or third-party services to conduct experiments and optimize your email campaigns for better performance.
- **Customer Relationship Management (CRM) Systems**: Integrate your email marketing platform with CRM systems such as Salesforce or HubSpot to track email interactions and performance metrics alongside other customer data.

- **Heatmapping Tools**: Use heatmapping tools such as Crazy Egg or Hotjar to visualize how recipients interact with your email content and identify areas for improvement.
- **Competitive Intelligence Tools**: Leverage competitive intelligence tools such as SimilarWeb or SEMrush to analyze the email marketing strategies and performance of your competitors.

Measuring and analyzing the performance of your email marketing campaigns is crucial for optimizing your strategies, improving engagement, and driving results. By tracking key metrics, employing analytical techniques, and utilizing appropriate tools, you can gain valuable insights into your audience's behavior, identify opportunities for optimization, and continuously improve the effectiveness of your email marketing efforts. Embrace a data-driven approach to email marketing performance analysis and use insights to inform your decisions and strategies moving forward.

6.1 Key Metrics to Track

Tracking key metrics is essential for evaluating the performance of your email marketing campaigns and identifying areas for improvement. By monitoring these metrics regularly, you can gain valuable insights into how your emails are performing and make data-driven decisions to optimize your strategies. Here are the key metrics you should track:

- **Open Rate**: The percentage of recipients who open your email out of the total number of emails delivered. The open rate indicates how effective your subject lines and sender name are at capturing recipients' attention and encouraging them to open your emails.

- **Click-Through Rate (CTR)**: The percentage of recipients who click on a link or call-to-action (CTA) within your email. CTR measures the effectiveness of your email content and design in driving engagement and directing recipients to your website or landing page.
- **Conversion Rate**: The percentage of recipients who complete a desired action, such as making a purchase, filling out a form, or downloading a resource, after clicking on a link in your email. The conversion rate reflects the effectiveness of your email in driving desired outcomes and achieving your campaign goals.
- **Bounce Rate**: The percentage of emails that were not successfully delivered to recipients' inboxes due to factors such as invalid email addresses, technical issues, or spam filters. Bounce rate measures the quality of your email list and the deliverability of your emails.
- **Unsubscribe Rate**: The percentage of recipients who opt out of receiving further emails from your mailing list after receiving a particular email. The unsubscribe rate indicates the level of dissatisfaction or disengagement among your subscribers and can help you assess the effectiveness of your email content and frequency.
- **List Growth Rate**: The rate at which your email list is growing over time. The list growth rate reflects your ability to attract new subscribers and maintain a healthy email list size, which is essential for the long-term success of your email marketing efforts.
- **Engagement Rate**: A composite metric that combines open rate, click-through rate, conversion rate, and other engagement metrics to measure overall subscriber engagement with your emails. Engagement rate provides a holistic view of how well your emails are performing and how actively your audience is interacting with your content.

By tracking these key metrics consistently and analyzing the trends and patterns in your email performance data, you can gain valuable insights into the effectiveness of your email marketing campaigns, identify areas for improvement, and optimize your strategies to drive better results.

6.2 A/B Testing for Optimization

A/B testing, also known as split testing, is a valuable technique used in email marketing to compare different versions of an email or specific elements within an email to determine which performs better in terms of engagement and conversion. By conducting A/B tests, marketers can gain valuable insights into their audience's preferences and behaviors and optimize their email campaigns for maximum effectiveness. Here's how A/B testing works and how to leverage it for optimization:

1. Identify Elements to Test

Start by identifying the elements within your emails that you want to test. Common elements to test include subject lines, sender names, email content, CTAs, images, layout, and send times. Choose elements that are likely to have a significant impact on engagement and conversion rates.

2. Create Variations

Create multiple variations of your email, each with a different version of the element you're testing. For example, if you're testing subject lines, create two or more versions of the subject line with different wording, length, or tone. Ensure that each variation differs only in the element you're testing to isolate its impact on performance.

3. Define Testing Parameters

Define the parameters of your A/B test, including the size of your test groups, the duration of the test, and the success metrics you'll use to evaluate performance. Ideally, split your email list randomly into equal-sized test groups to ensure statistical validity and accuracy in your results.

4. Run the Test

Send each variation of your email to its respective test group and track the performance metrics you're testing, such as open rates, click-through rates, conversion rates, or engagement rates. Monitor the results in real-time or over the specified test period to gather sufficient data for analysis.

5. Analyze Results

Once the test is complete, analyze the results to determine which variation performed better in terms of your chosen success metric. Compare the performance of each variation statistically using confidence intervals or significance testing to ensure the results are statistically significant and not due to random chance.

6. Implement Winning Variation

Based on the results of your A/B test, implement the winning variation into your ongoing email campaigns. Use the insights gained from the test to optimize future campaigns and iterate on your strategies to improve performance continually.

7. Iterate and Test Again

A/B testing is an iterative process, and ongoing testing and optimization are essential for maximizing the effectiveness of your email marketing campaigns. Continuously test different elements and variations to refine your strategies, learn more about your audience, and drive better results over time.

By leveraging A/B testing for optimization, marketers can make data-driven decisions, improve the performance of their email campaigns, and ultimately achieve their business objectives more effectively. A/B testing empowers marketers to identify what resonates best with their audience and continuously refine their strategies for maximum impact and ROI.

6.3 Analyzing Campaign Performance

Analyzing campaign performance is crucial for understanding the effectiveness of your email marketing efforts and identifying opportunities for optimization. By evaluating key metrics and identifying trends in your data, you can make informed decisions to improve future campaigns and drive better results. Here's how to effectively analyze campaign performance:

1. Review Key Metrics

Start by reviewing key metrics such as open rates, click-through rates, conversion rates, bounce rates, unsubscribe rates, and engagement rates. These metrics provide valuable insights into how recipients are interacting with your emails and can help you gauge the overall success of your campaigns.

2. Identify Trends and Patterns

Look for trends and patterns in your data by comparing performance metrics across different campaigns, segments, or periods. Identify which campaigns performed exceptionally well and which ones underperformed, and try to understand the factors that contributed to their success or failure.

3. Segmentation Analysis

Segment your data by factors such as demographics, behaviors, or lifecycle stages to gain deeper insights into how different audience segments are responding to your emails. Analyze performance metrics for each segment to identify patterns and tailor your strategies accordingly.

4. A/B Test Results

Review the results of any A/B tests or experiments you conducted as part of your campaigns. Identify which variations performed better and use the insights gained to optimize future campaigns and refine your email marketing strategies.

5. Lifecycle Analysis

Track the performance of your emails throughout the customer lifecycle, from acquisition to conversion to retention. Analyze how engagement and conversion rates vary at each stage of the customer journey and identify opportunities to improve the effectiveness of your email campaigns at each stage.

6. ROI Analysis

Calculate the return on investment (ROI) of your email marketing campaigns by comparing the revenue generated from email conversions to the costs associated with email marketing. Evaluate the financial performance of your campaigns and assess their contribution to your overall business objectives.

7. Competitive Analysis

Benchmark your email performance against competitors or industry benchmarks to gain insights into your relative performance and identify areas where you can improve. Analyze factors such as average open rates, click-through rates, and conversion rates to understand how you stack up against the competition.

8. Customer Feedback

Collect feedback from recipients through surveys, feedback forms, or direct communication channels to gain insights into their preferences, needs, and expectations. Use customer feedback to inform your email marketing strategies and ensure they resonate with your audience.

9. Iterate and Improve

Based on your analysis, identify areas for improvement and develop actionable insights to optimize your email marketing campaigns. Continuously iterate on your strategies, test new ideas, and measure the impact of your optimizations to drive continuous improvement in campaign performance.

By systematically analyzing campaign performance and leveraging insights gained from your data, you can refine your email marketing strategies, enhance engagement with your audience, and achieve better results over time. Embrace a data-driven approach to campaign analysis and use insights to inform your decisions and strategies moving forward.

6.4 Leveraging Data for Continuous Improvement

Data plays a pivotal role in driving continuous improvement in email marketing campaigns. By harnessing the power of data analytics, marketers can gain valuable insights into audience behavior, campaign performance, and market trends, enabling them to make informed decisions and optimize their strategies for better results. Here's how to leverage data effectively for continuous improvement:

1. Collect Comprehensive Data

Start by collecting comprehensive data on various aspects of your email marketing campaigns, including recipient demographics, engagement metrics, conversion rates, and revenue generated. Use tracking tools, analytics platforms, and CRM systems to gather data from multiple sources and ensure you have a complete view of your campaign performance.

2. Monitor Key Performance Metrics

Regularly monitor key performance metrics such as open rates, click-through rates, conversion rates, and ROI to track the effectiveness of your email campaigns. Set up automated reports or dashboards to track metrics in real time and identify any fluctuations or trends that require attention.

3. Segmentation and Personalization

Utilize data segmentation to divide your audience into distinct groups based on demographics, behaviors, or preferences. Leverage personalization techniques to tailor your email content and offers to the specific needs and interests of each segment. Analyze the performance of segmented campaigns to identify which segments are most responsive and refine your targeting strategies accordingly.

4. A/B Testing and Experimentation

Conduct A/B tests and experiments to test different elements of your emails, such as subject lines, content, CTAs, and send times. Analyze the results of your tests to identify winning variations and insights that can inform future campaign optimizations. Continuously iterate on your strategies based on test results to improve performance over time.

5. Lifecycle Marketing

Implement lifecycle marketing strategies to engage with subscribers at different stages of the customer journey, from acquisition to retention. Use data to identify where subscribers are in the lifecycle and deliver targeted messages and offers that align with their needs and behaviors. Analyze the effectiveness of lifecycle campaigns in nurturing leads, driving conversions, and fostering customer loyalty.

6. Predictive Analytics

Harness the power of predictive analytics and machine learning algorithms to anticipate future trends and behaviors based on historical data patterns. Use predictive models to identify high-value segments, forecast campaign performance, and optimize targeting and messaging strategies for maximum impact.

7. Continuous Optimization

Embrace a culture of continuous optimization by regularly reviewing campaign performance, identifying areas for improvement, and implementing iterative changes based on data-driven insights. Experiment with new ideas, technologies, and strategies to stay ahead of evolving trends and maintain a competitive edge in the market.

8. Benchmarking and Competitive Analysis

Benchmark your campaign performance against industry benchmarks and competitors to assess your relative performance and identify opportunities for improvement. Analyze competitor strategies, tactics, and messaging to gain insights into emerging best practices and areas where you can differentiate and innovate.

Embrace a data-driven approach to email marketing, and use insights gained from data analysis to inform your decisions and strategies, driving continuous optimization and innovation in your campaigns.

Chapter 7: Advanced Strategies and Integration

In this chapter, we delve into advanced strategies and integration techniques that can elevate your email marketing efforts to new heights. By incorporating these advanced strategies and integrating your email marketing with other channels and technologies, you can unlock additional opportunities for engagement, personalization, and conversion.

1. Advanced Segmentation and Personalization

Explore advanced segmentation techniques to create highly targeted and personalized email campaigns. Utilize data-driven segmentation based on customer behavior, purchase history, browsing activity, and engagement levels to tailor your messaging and offers to the unique preferences and interests of individual recipients. Leverage dynamic content and predictive analytics to deliver hyper-personalized experiences that resonate with each recipient on a deeper level.

2. Automation and Behavioral Triggers

Harness the power of automation and behavioral triggers to deliver timely and relevant messages to your audience. Set up automated workflows triggered by specific actions or events, such as website visits, email interactions, or purchase behaviors, to nurture leads, re-engage inactive subscribers, and drive conversions. Use behavioral triggers to deliver personalized messages based on recipient actions and preferences, increasing engagement and driving results.

3. Multichannel Integration

Integrate your email marketing efforts with other marketing channels, such as social media, SMS, and push notifications, to create cohesive and integrated campaigns that reach your audience across multiple touchpoints. Coordinate messaging and offers across channels to provide a seamless and consistent experience for your audience, driving engagement and conversion across the customer journey.

4. Advanced Analytics and Data Insights

Utilize advanced analytics and data insights to gain a deeper understanding of your audience and campaign performance. Leverage predictive analytics, machine learning, and AI-driven algorithms to forecast future trends, identify high-value segments, and optimize targeting and messaging strategies for maximum impact. Dive into granular data analysis to uncover actionable insights and opportunities for optimization, driving continuous improvement in your email marketing efforts.

5. Personalized Content Experiences

Deliver personalized content experiences that captivate and engage your audience. Experiment with interactive content, video marketing, and immersive storytelling techniques to create compelling and memorable experiences that resonate with recipients. Tailor content to the preferences and interests of individual recipients, leveraging user-generated content, user-generated reviews, and personalized recommendations to enhance engagement and drive conversion.

6. Lifecycle Marketing and Customer Journeys

Implement lifecycle marketing strategies to guide customers through the entire customer journey, from awareness to advocacy. Map out customer journeys and create targeted email campaigns that address the needs and preferences of customers at each stage of the lifecycle. Use data-driven insights to identify opportunities for upselling, cross-selling, and retention, driving long-term customer loyalty and lifetime value.

7. Integration with Marketing Automation Platforms

Integrate your email marketing with marketing automation platforms to streamline workflows, optimize processes, and scale your efforts effectively. Leverage advanced automation capabilities, such as lead scoring, lead nurturing, and drip campaigns, to automate repetitive tasks and deliver personalized experiences at scale. Integrate with CRM systems to sync customer data and insights across platforms, enabling seamless communication and coordination across the marketing stack.

By implementing advanced strategies and integrating your email marketing with other channels and technologies, you can unlock new opportunities for engagement, personalization, and conversion. Embrace innovation, experimentation, and continuous optimization to stay ahead of the curve and drive results in today's dynamic and competitive landscape.

7.1 Integrating Email with Social Media and Other Channels

Integrating email marketing with social media and other channels can amplify your reach, enhance engagement, and create cohesive marketing campaigns that resonate with your audience across multiple touchpoints. By leveraging the strengths of each channel and orchestrating cross-channel interactions, you can maximize the impact of your marketing efforts and drive better results. Here's how to integrate email with social media and other channels effectively:

1. Cross-promotion and Coordinated Messaging

Promote your email campaigns on social media channels and vice versa to increase visibility and drive traffic to your content. Share teasers, highlights, or exclusive offers from your emails on social media platforms to generate interest and encourage subscribers to engage with your content. Likewise, include social media icons and links in your emails to encourage recipients to follow your brand and engage with your content on social media.

2. Consistent Branding and Messaging

Maintain consistent branding and messaging across email and social media channels to provide a seamless and cohesive experience for your audience. Ensure that your brand voice, visual identity, and messaging align across all channels to reinforce brand recognition and build trust with your audience. Coordinate campaign themes, promotions, and messaging strategies to create a unified brand experience across email, social media, and other channels.

3. Cross-Channel Engagement Campaigns

Develop cross-channel engagement campaigns that leverage the unique strengths of each channel to drive interaction and participation from your audience. For example, run contests, polls, or giveaways on social media and promote them via email to encourage participation and increase engagement across channels. Use email to follow up with participants, share results, and nurture leads generated from social media campaigns.

4. Social Sharing and Referral Programs

Encourage social sharing and word-of-mouth referrals by incorporating social sharing buttons and referral incentives into your email campaigns. Make it easy for recipients to share your emails or refer friends and family to your brand via social media, email, or other channels. Offer incentives such as discounts, rewards, or exclusive content to incentivize sharing and drive viral growth of your campaigns.

5. Targeted Advertising and Retargeting

Use email subscriber data to inform targeted advertising and retargeting campaigns on social media and other digital channels. Leverage custom audiences, lookalike audiences, and retargeting pixels to reach subscribers with relevant ads based on their interests, behaviors, and interactions with your brand. Coordinate messaging and offers across email and advertising channels to create a cohesive and personalized experience for your audience.

6. Integration with Marketing Automation Platforms

Integrate your email marketing platform with marketing automation platforms to synchronize data, workflows, and campaigns across channels seamlessly. Leverage automation rules, triggers, and workflows to orchestrate cross-channel interactions and deliver personalized experiences based on customer behavior and preferences. Use data-driven insights from email and other channels to optimize targeting, timing, and messaging strategies for maximum impact.

7. Performance Tracking and Attribution

Track the performance of your integrated campaigns across email, social media, and other channels to measure their effectiveness and impact on key metrics such as engagement, conversion, and ROI. Use multi-touch attribution models to understand how interactions across channels contribute to conversions and customer journeys. Analyze cross-channel performance data to identify opportunities for optimization and refinement of your integrated marketing strategies.

By integrating email with social media and other channels, you can create seamless and cohesive marketing campaigns that engage your audience across multiple touchpoints and drive better results. Embrace cross-channel integration, coordination, and optimization to maximize the impact of your marketing efforts and achieve your business objectives effectively.

7.2 Leveraging AI and Machine Learning in Email Marketing

Harnessing the power of artificial intelligence (AI) and machine learning (ML) can revolutionize your email marketing efforts, enabling you to deliver more personalized, relevant, and engaging experiences to your audience. By leveraging AI and ML technologies, you can automate repetitive tasks, optimize targeting and messaging, and unlock valuable insights from your data. Here's how to leverage AI and machine learning in email marketing effectively:

1. Personalization at Scale

Use AI-powered algorithms to analyze customer data and behavior patterns, allowing you to deliver highly personalized email content and offers to each recipient. Leverage dynamic content generation, predictive analytics, and recommendation engines to tailor email content, product recommendations, and promotional offers based on individual preferences, interests, and past interactions.

2. Predictive Analytics for Segmentation

Utilize predictive analytics to segment your audience dynamically and identify high-value segments with similar characteristics and behaviors. Leverage clustering algorithms, propensity models, and customer lifetime value predictions to segment your audience based on factors such as purchase history, engagement levels, and predicted future behaviors. Use these segments to target your emails more effectively and drive better results.

3. Automated Email Workflows

Implement AI-driven automation workflows to streamline your email marketing processes and deliver timely, relevant messages to your audience. Use machine learning algorithms to analyze customer journeys and trigger automated emails based on specific actions, behaviors, or lifecycle stages. Leverage automation rules, triggers, and decision trees to orchestrate personalized email sequences that nurture leads, re-engage inactive subscribers, and drive conversions.

4. Smart Subject Line Optimization

Utilize AI-powered tools to optimize email subject lines for maximum impact and engagement. Leverage natural language processing (NLP) algorithms to analyze subject line performance data and identify patterns, keywords, and language cues that resonate with your audience. Use A/B testing and predictive modeling to experiment with different subject line variations and predict which ones are most likely to drive opens and clicks.

5. Content Generation and Optimization

Employ AI-powered content generation tools to create compelling email content quickly and efficiently. Use natural language generation (NLG) algorithms to generate personalized product recommendations, dynamic email copy, and tailored messaging based on customer data and preferences. Leverage machine learning algorithms to optimize email content for readability, relevance, and engagement, ensuring that each email resonates with recipients and drives action.

6. Real-time Email Analytics and Insights

Utilize AI-driven analytics platforms to gain real-time insights into email performance and audience behavior. Leverage machine learning algorithms to analyze email engagement metrics, predict future trends, and identify opportunities for optimization. Use advanced data visualization techniques, anomaly detection, and predictive modeling to uncover actionable insights and make data-driven decisions to improve your email marketing strategies.

7. Spam Detection and Deliverability

Utilize AI-powered spam detection algorithms to ensure that your emails reach recipients' inboxes and avoid being flagged as spam. Leverage machine learning techniques to analyze email content, sender reputation, and engagement signals to predict deliverability and optimize email deliverability rates. Use AI-driven deliverability tools and monitoring systems to identify and address deliverability issues proactively, ensuring that your emails reach their intended audience effectively.

By leveraging AI and machine learning in your email marketing efforts, you can unlock new opportunities for personalization, automation, and optimization, driving better results and enhancing the overall customer experience. Embrace AI-powered technologies and tools to streamline your processes, deliver more relevant content, and achieve your business objectives more effectively in today's dynamic and competitive landscape.

7.3 Implementing Interactive and Dynamic Content

Integrating interactive and dynamic content into your email marketing campaigns can captivate your audience, drive engagement, and increase conversion rates. By leveraging interactive elements and dynamic content, you can create immersive and personalized experiences that resonate with recipients and encourage action. Here's how to implement interactive and dynamic content effectively in your email marketing:

1. Interactive Elements

Incorporate interactive elements such as buttons, carousels, accordions, quizzes, polls, and surveys into your email campaigns to encourage engagement and interaction. Allow recipients to click, swipe, or interact with content directly within the email to explore products, view additional information, or provide feedback. Use interactive elements strategically to enhance the user experience and drive desired actions, such as clicks, conversions, or sign-ups.

2. Animated GIFs and Videos

Use animated GIFs and videos to add visual interest and excitement to your email content. Incorporate eye-catching animations, product demos, or explainer videos to grab attention and convey your message effectively. Use animated GIFs and videos to showcase product features, highlight promotions, or tell a story that resonates with your audience. Ensure that videos are optimized for email and compatible with email clients to ensure a seamless viewing experience.

3. Personalized Recommendations

Utilize dynamic content blocks to deliver personalized product recommendations and tailored offers to each recipient based on their preferences, purchase history, and browsing behavior. Use machine learning algorithms to analyze customer data and predict which products or services are most relevant to each recipient. Dynamically populate email content with personalized recommendations to increase relevance and drive conversions.

4. Countdown Timers and Live Content Updates

Incorporate countdown timers and live content updates into your email campaigns to create a sense of urgency and encourage immediate action. Use countdown timers to highlight limited-time offers, flash sales, or upcoming events, prompting recipients to act quickly to take advantage of the offer. Utilize live content updates to dynamically update email content based on real-time data, such as inventory levels, event schedules, or weather conditions, ensuring that recipients receive the most up-to-date information.

5. Dynamic Content Personalization

Implement dynamic content personalization to tailor email content and messaging to the preferences and interests of each recipient. Use merge tags, conditional logic, and dynamic content blocks to customize email content based on demographic data, purchase history, geographic location, or behavioral segments. Deliver targeted messages and offers that resonate with each recipient, increasing engagement and driving conversions.

6. User-generated Content and Social Feeds

Incorporate user-generated content (UGC) and social media feeds into your email campaigns to showcase authentic customer experiences and foster community engagement. Curate UGC such as customer reviews, testimonials, or social media posts and feature them prominently in your emails to build trust and credibility with recipients. Embed live social media feeds or hashtags into your emails to encourage recipients to join the conversation and interact with your brand on social media.

7. Interactive Surveys and Feedback Forms

Engage recipients with interactive surveys, quizzes, or feedback forms embedded directly within your email campaigns. Encourage recipients to provide feedback, answer questions, or participate in polls to gather valuable insights and feedback from your audience. Use interactive surveys and feedback forms to gather customer preferences, gauge satisfaction levels, and tailor future email campaigns to better meet the needs of your audience.

By implementing interactive and dynamic content in your email marketing campaigns, you can create immersive, personalized experiences that resonate with recipients and drive meaningful engagement and action. Experiment with different interactive elements and dynamic content strategies to find what resonates best with your audience and enhances the effectiveness of your email marketing efforts.

7.4 Future Trends in Email Marketing

As technology continues to evolve and consumer preferences shift, the landscape of email marketing is constantly evolving. To stay ahead of the curve and drive success in the future, it's essential to keep an eye on emerging trends and adapt your strategies accordingly. Here are some future trends in email marketing to watch out for:

1. **Artificial Intelligence and Machine Learning**

The integration of artificial intelligence (AI) and machine learning (ML) technologies will continue to transform email marketing. AI-powered tools will enable marketers to automate processes, personalize content at scale, and deliver predictive insights to optimize campaign performance. Machine learning algorithms will analyze data to uncover patterns, predict customer behavior, and enhance targeting and segmentation strategies.

2.   Hyper-Personalization

Hyper-personalization will become the norm in email marketing, with marketers leveraging advanced data analytics and AI-driven algorithms to deliver highly tailored and relevant content to individual recipients. Personalization will extend beyond basic segmentation to include dynamic content blocks, real-time recommendations, and contextual messaging based on factors such as past behavior, preferences, and location.

3.   Interactive and Dynamic Content

Interactive and dynamic content will play a central role in email marketing, with marketers leveraging animated GIFs, videos, interactive elements, and dynamic content blocks to create engaging and immersive experiences for recipients. Interactive emails will enable recipients to interact with content directly within the email, increasing engagement and driving higher conversion rates.

4.   Mobile Optimization and Responsive Design

With the majority of email opens occurring on mobile devices, mobile optimization, and responsive design will remain critical for email marketing success. Marketers will focus on creating mobile-friendly email templates, optimizing content for small screens, and leveraging mobile-specific features such as click-to-call buttons and mobile wallets to enhance the mobile user experience.

5. Privacy and Data Protection

In light of increasing privacy concerns and regulatory changes such as GDPR and CCPA, marketers will need to prioritize data protection and compliance in their email marketing practices. Transparency, consent management, and data security will be paramount, with marketers adopting stricter measures to safeguard customer data and ensure compliance with regulations.

6. Automation and Workflow Orchestration

Automation and workflow orchestration will enable marketers to streamline processes, deliver timely messages, and nurture leads throughout the customer journey. Marketers will leverage automation tools to create personalized email sequences, trigger messages based on specific actions or behaviors, and automate repetitive tasks to improve efficiency and scalability.

7. Integration with Omnichannel Strategies

Email marketing will be integrated more closely with omnichannel marketing strategies, with marketers orchestrating seamless experiences across multiple touchpoints and channels. Integration with social media, SMS, push notifications, and other channels will enable marketers to deliver cohesive messaging and personalized experiences that resonate with customers throughout their journey.

8. Voice and Conversational Marketing

As voice technology continues to gain traction, marketers will explore new opportunities for voice-enabled email experiences and conversational marketing. Voice-activated email assistants, voice search optimization, and conversational AI chatbots will enable marketers to engage with customers in more natural and interactive ways, driving engagement and fostering deeper connections with recipients.

9. Sustainability and Ethical Practices

Sustainability and ethical practices will become increasingly important considerations in email marketing, with marketers prioritizing environmentally friendly practices, ethical data usage, and corporate social responsibility. Marketers will focus on reducing email waste, minimizing carbon emissions, and promoting sustainable products and initiatives to align with consumer values and expectations.

10. Continuous Innovation and Experimentation

Innovation and experimentation will be key drivers of success in email marketing, with marketers embracing new technologies, trends, and strategies to stay ahead of the competition. Continuous testing, optimization, and adaptation will be essential as marketers strive to deliver innovative, relevant, and impactful email experiences that resonate with their audience and drive business results.

By staying abreast of these future trends and adapting your email marketing strategies accordingly, you can position your brand for success in the evolving landscape of digital marketing. Embrace innovation, experimentation, and customer-centricity to stay ahead of the curve and drive meaningful engagement and results through email marketing.

Chapter 8: Case Studies and Practical Examples

In this chapter, we'll explore real-world case studies and practical examples that illustrate successful email marketing strategies, tactics, and campaigns. By examining these case studies, you'll gain valuable insights into how leading brands and marketers leverage email marketing to drive engagement, nurture leads, and achieve business objectives. Let's dive into some inspiring examples:

1. Airbnb: Personalized Recommendations

Airbnb leverages personalized recommendations in its email marketing campaigns to provide tailored travel experiences to its customers. By analyzing user behavior, preferences, and past bookings, Airbnb delivers targeted email recommendations for accommodations, experiences, and destinations that align with each recipient's interests and travel history. This personalized approach enhances customer satisfaction, increases booking rates, and fosters loyalty among Airbnb users.

2. Casper: Interactive Content

Mattress Company Casper incorporates interactive content into their email marketing campaigns to engage recipients and drive conversions. Casper's emails feature interactive elements such as product quizzes, sleep assessments, and interactive videos that allow recipients to engage with content directly within the email. This interactive approach not only increases email engagement but also educates customers about Casper's products and helps them make informed purchasing decisions.

3. Netflix: Triggered Emails

Streaming giant Netflix uses triggered emails to re-engage inactive subscribers and encourage them to resume their subscriptions. Netflix sends personalized emails to users who haven't watched content in a while, highlighting new releases, recommended shows, or exclusive content based on their viewing history and preferences. These triggered emails remind users of the value of their Netflix subscription and prompt them to return to the platform, reducing churn and increasing retention rates.

4. Dollar Shave Club: Clever Copywriting

Dollar Shave Club differentiates itself with witty copywriting in its email marketing campaigns. The company's emails feature clever subject lines, playful language, and humorous imagery that resonate with its target audience and set it apart from competitors. Dollar Shave Club's lighthearted approach to email marketing helps build brand affinity, drive engagement, and foster a sense of community among its subscribers.

5. Warby Parker: Customer Stories

Eyewear retailer Warby Parker incorporates customer stories and testimonials into its email marketing to build trust and social proof. Warby Parker's emails feature real customer testimonials, photos, and reviews highlighting positive experiences with the brand's products and customer service. By showcasing authentic customer stories, Warby

Parker reinforces its brand reputation, alleviates purchase anxiety, and encourages conversions among potential customers.

6.   HubSpot: Educational Content

Marketing software company HubSpot provides valuable educational content in its email marketing campaigns to educate, inform, and empower its audience. HubSpot's emails include blog posts, ebooks, webinars, and other resources that address common pain points, challenges, and questions faced by its target audience. By delivering actionable insights and practical advice, HubSpot establishes itself as a trusted authority in its industry and nurtures leads through the buyer's journey.

7.   Nike: Limited-Time Offers

Sportswear giant Nike uses limited-time offers and exclusive promotions to create urgency and drive sales through email marketing. Nike's emails feature time-sensitive deals, flash sales, and limited-edition product releases that encourage recipients to act quickly to take advantage of the offer. By leveraging scarcity and FOMO (fear of missing out), Nike motivates customers to make purchases and drive revenue through its email campaigns.

8.   Starbucks: Personalized Rewards

Coffee chain Starbucks utilizes personalized rewards and offers in its email marketing to incentivize loyalty and drive repeat purchases.

Starbucks' emails contain personalized offers, discounts, and rewards tailored to each recipient's purchase history, preferences, and loyalty status. By rewarding customer loyalty and providing exclusive benefits, Starbucks strengthens customer relationships, increases customer lifetime value, and drives sales both online and in-store.

9. Trello: Onboarding Emails

Project management tool Trello employs strategic onboarding emails to educate new users and drive product adoption. Trello's onboarding emails guide users through the platform's features, functionalities, and best practices, helping them get started and maximize their productivity. By providing valuable tips, tutorials, and resources, Trello ensures a smooth user experience, reduces churn, and fosters long-term engagement with its platform.

10. Amazon: Personalized Recommendations and Retargeting

E-commerce giant Amazon excels in email marketing with personalized product recommendations and retargeting campaigns. Amazon's emails feature personalized product suggestions based on each recipient's browsing history, purchase behavior, and shopping preferences. Additionally, Amazon employs retargeting emails to remind users of items left in their shopping cart or viewed but not purchased, encouraging them to complete the purchase and drive conversion.

By studying these case studies and practical examples, you can gain valuable insights into effective email marketing strategies, tactics, and techniques employed by leading brands and marketers. Use these insights to inform and inspire your email marketing campaigns, experiment with new ideas, and continuously optimize your strategies to drive engagement, nurture leads, and achieve your business goals.

8.1 Successful Email Campaigns from Leading Brands

In this section, we'll explore some notable examples of successful email campaigns from leading brands across various industries. These campaigns have achieved remarkable results in terms of engagement, conversion, and brand awareness, showcasing effective strategies and tactics that you can draw inspiration from for your email marketing efforts. Let's delve into these inspiring case studies:

1. **Nike: Personalized Product Recommendations**

Nike's email campaigns leverage personalized product recommendations based on customers' browsing and purchase history. By analyzing user behavior and preferences, Nike delivers tailored recommendations for footwear, apparel, and accessories that align with each recipient's interests and style preferences. This personalized approach enhances customer engagement, increases click-through rates, and drives conversions by showcasing relevant products that resonate with recipients.

2. **Starbucks: Loyalty Program Rewards and Offers**

Starbucks' email campaigns feature exclusive rewards, discounts, and offers for members of its loyalty program, Starbucks Rewards. These emails provide personalized offers based on customers' purchase history, reward status, and location, incentivizing repeat purchases and driving customer loyalty. Starbucks' strategic use of targeted offers and rewards encourages customers to visit its stores more frequently, increasing sales and fostering long-term relationships with its audience.

3. Amazon: Cart Abandonment Retargeting

Amazon excels in email marketing with its cart abandonment retargeting campaigns, which remind users of items left in their shopping cart and encourage them to complete the purchase. Amazon's emails include personalized product recommendations, customer reviews, and incentives such as discounts or free shipping to incentivize recipients to return to the site and finalize their purchase. This retargeting strategy helps recover lost sales, reduce cart abandonment rates, and drive revenue for the e-commerce giant.

4. Airbnb: Personalized Travel Recommendations

Airbnb's email campaigns deliver personalized travel recommendations and destination inspiration to users based on their past bookings, search history, and preferences. Airbnb's emails feature curated lists of accommodations, experiences, and destinations tailored to each recipient's interests, travel history, and budget. This personalized approach enhances the user experience, encourages repeat bookings, and drives revenue for Airbnb by showcasing relevant and appealing travel options to recipients.

5. HubSpot: Educational Content and Thought Leadership

HubSpot's email marketing strategy focuses on providing valuable educational content and thought leadership to its audience. HubSpot's emails include blog posts, ebooks, webinars, and other resources that address common pain points, challenges, and questions faced by marketers and businesses. By delivering actionable insights and practical advice, HubSpot establishes itself as a trusted authority in its industry, drives engagement with its brand, and nurtures leads through the buyer's journey.

6. Dollar Shave Club: Clever and Engaging Copywriting

Dollar Shave Club stands out with its witty and engaging copywriting in its email campaigns. The company's emails feature humorous subject lines, playful language, and creative imagery that resonate with its target audience and set it apart from competitors. Dollar Shave Club's lighthearted approach to email marketing helps build brand affinity, drive engagement, and foster a sense of community among its subscribers, leading to increased customer loyalty and brand advocacy.

7. Trello: Onboarding and User Education

Trello's email marketing strategy focuses on user onboarding and education, providing valuable resources and guidance to new users to help them get started and maximize their productivity with the platform. Trello's onboarding emails include tutorials, tips, and best practices for using its project management tool effectively. By offering practical advice and support, Trello ensures a positive user experience, reduces churn, and fosters long-term engagement and loyalty among its user base.

8.   Netflix: Personalized Content Recommendations

Netflix uses personalized content recommendations in its email campaigns to re-engage inactive subscribers and encourage them to return to the platform. Netflix's emails highlight new releases, recommended shows, or exclusive content based on each recipient's viewing history, preferences, and behavior. By delivering personalized recommendations that align with users' interests, Netflix entices recipients to rediscover content they love, reducing churn and increasing retention rates for the streaming service.

9.   Warby Parker: Customer Stories and Social Proof

Eyewear retailer Warby Parker incorporates customer stories and social proof into its email marketing to build trust and credibility with its audience. Warby Parker's emails feature real customer testimonials, photos, and reviews highlighting positive experiences with its products and customer service. By showcasing authentic customer stories, Warby Parker reinforces its brand reputation, alleviates purchase anxiety, and encourages conversions among potential customers.

10. Casper: Interactive Content and Engagement

Mattress Company Casper uses interactive content in its email campaigns to engage recipients and drive conversions. Casper's emails feature interactive elements such as product quizzes, sleep assessments, and interactive videos that allow recipients to engage with content directly within the email. This interactive approach not only increases email engagement but also educates customers about Casper's products and helps them make informed purchasing decisions.

By studying these successful email campaigns from leading brands, you can gain valuable insights into effective strategies, tactics, and techniques for driving engagement, nurturing leads, and achieving business objectives through email marketing. Use these examples as inspiration to inform and optimize your email marketing efforts, experiment with new ideas, and continuously improve your strategies to deliver meaningful results for your brand.

8.2 Small Business Success Stories

While large corporations often dominate discussions about successful email marketing, small businesses have also achieved remarkable results with strategic and creative email campaigns. In this section, we'll explore some inspiring success stories from small businesses that demonstrate the power of email marketing in driving growth, engagement, and customer loyalty. Let's dive into these compelling examples:

1. **Local Bakery: Personalized Promotions and Offers**

A small bakery in a local community used email marketing to drive foot traffic and increase sales. By collecting email addresses from in-store customers and website visitors, the bakery built a loyal subscriber base. They sent personalized email promotions, such as discounts on birthday cakes or special offers for holidays like Valentine's Day or Mother's Day. These targeted campaigns not only drove repeat business from existing customers but also attracted new customers who were enticed by the enticing offers.

2. **Online Boutique: Seasonal Lookbooks and Style Guides**

An online boutique specializing in fashion and accessories used email marketing to showcase new arrivals and seasonal collections. They sent out regular emails featuring curated lookbooks, style guides, and outfit inspiration, catering to different customer preferences and fashion trends. By providing valuable content and product recommendations, the boutique engaged its audience, drove website traffic, and increased sales of featured products.

3. **Fitness Studio: Class Reminders and Special Events**

A local fitness studio utilized email marketing to keep members informed about class schedules, special events, and promotions. They sent out weekly newsletters with class reminders, workout tips, and motivational messages to encourage attendance and engagement. Additionally, they promoted special events such as workshops, challenges, and member appreciation days via email, driving participation and fostering a sense of community among members.

4. Freelance Photographer: Portfolio Showcases and Client Testimonials

A freelance photographer leveraged email marketing to showcase their portfolio and attract new clients. They regularly sent out email newsletters featuring highlights from recent photo shoots, client testimonials, and behind-the-scenes stories. By showcasing their work and sharing positive feedback from satisfied clients, the photographer built credibility, generated leads, and secured bookings for future projects.

5. Local Coffee Shop: Exclusive Offers and Loyalty Rewards

A neighborhood coffee shop used email marketing to reward loyal customers and drive repeat business. They implemented a loyalty program where customers could sign up for exclusive offers and discounts via email. Additionally, they sent out monthly newsletters with updates on new menu items, upcoming events, and community initiatives. By offering personalized rewards and fostering a sense of belonging, the coffee shop built customer loyalty and increased customer retention.

6. Consulting Firm: Thought Leadership Content and Industry Insights

A small consulting firm specializing in marketing and business strategy used email marketing to position themselves as thought leaders in their industry. They regularly sent out email newsletters with insightful articles, case studies, and industry trends to their subscriber list. By providing valuable content that addressed common challenges and provided actionable advice, the consulting firm established credibility, attracted leads, and ultimately secured new clients.

7. Handmade Crafts Store: DIY Tutorials and Product Showcases

An artisanal crafts store utilized email marketing to showcase their handmade products and inspire creativity among their audience. They sent out weekly emails featuring DIY tutorials, craft ideas, and product showcases, encouraging recipients to explore their creative side and consider purchasing handmade gifts or supplies. By providing valuable content and promoting their products in a subtle yet compelling way, the crafts store increased brand awareness and drove sales.

8. Local Restaurant: Weekly Specials and Events

A family-owned restaurant used email marketing to promote weekly specials, events, and promotions to its loyal customer base. They sent out weekly emails with mouthwatering photos of featured dishes, chef's recommendations, and details about upcoming events such as live music nights or themed dinners. By staying top-of-mind and enticing customers with tempting offers, the restaurant boosted foot traffic, increased table reservations, and cultivated a loyal following among local diners.

9. Artisanal Bakery: Recipe Ideas and Baking Tips

An artisanal bakery employed email marketing to engage with its audience and showcase its passion for baking. They sent out bi-weekly emails featuring recipe ideas, baking tips, and stories behind their artisanal creations. Additionally, they promoted seasonal specials and limited-edition products via email, creating a sense of excitement and anticipation among their subscribers. By sharing their expertise and inviting customers to join them on their baking journey, the bakery fostered a strong connection with its audience and drove sales.

10. Home Services Provider: Seasonal Maintenance Reminders and Tips

A local home services provider used email marketing to stay connected with its customers and provide valuable maintenance tips and reminders. They sent out quarterly emails with seasonal home maintenance checklists, energy-saving tips, and exclusive offers for HVAC servicing or plumbing inspections. By proactively reaching out to customers and offering helpful advice, the home services provider positioned itself as a trusted advisor, increased customer loyalty, and generated repeat business.

These small business success stories demonstrate the versatility and effectiveness of email marketing in driving growth, engagement, and customer loyalty across diverse industries and niches. By adopting strategic approaches, providing valuable content, and leveraging the power of email communication, small businesses can achieve remarkable results and compete effectively in today's competitive marketplace.

8.3 Lessons Learned and Best Practices

After exploring successful email marketing campaigns from leading brands and small businesses, several key lessons and best practices emerge. Whether you're a large corporation or a small business, these insights can inform your email marketing strategy and help you achieve your goals effectively. Let's delve into some of the most important lessons learned and best practices:

1. **Know Your Audience**

Understanding your audience is paramount to the success of your email marketing efforts. Take the time to segment your audience based on demographics, interests, and behaviors to deliver targeted and relevant content that resonates with recipients.

2. **Personalization is Key**

Personalization can significantly impact the effectiveness of your email campaigns. Tailor your content, offers, and messaging to each recipient's preferences, past interactions, and purchase history to create a personalized experience that fosters engagement and drives conversions.

3. Provide Value

Focus on providing value to your subscribers in every email you send. Whether it's informative content, exclusive offers, or entertaining stories, ensure that your emails deliver something of value to recipients and enhance their experience with your brand.

4. Be Creative and Engaging

Stand out from the crowd with creative and engaging email content. Experiment with interactive elements, compelling visuals, and clever copywriting to capture recipients' attention and encourage interaction with your emails.

5. Test and Iterate

Continuously test and optimize your email campaigns to maximize their effectiveness. Experiment with different subject lines, content formats, and calls-to-action to identify what resonates best with your audience and refine your approach accordingly.

6. Mobile Optimization is Essential

With the majority of email opens occurring on mobile devices, ensure that your emails are optimized for mobile viewing. Use responsive design, clear and concise formatting, and large, clickable buttons to create a seamless and user-friendly experience for mobile users.

7. Compliance and Transparency

Adhere to best practices and regulatory requirements to ensure compliance with laws such as GDPR and CAN-SPAM. Obtain proper consent from recipients before sending marketing emails, provide clear opt-out options, and be transparent about how you collect, use, and protect their personal data.

8. Measure and Analyze Performance

Track key metrics such as open rates, click-through rates, and conversion rates to gauge the effectiveness of your email campaigns. Use analytics tools to gain insights into recipient behavior, identify areas for improvement, and make data-driven decisions to optimize your strategies.

9. Maintain Consistency and Frequency

Maintain a consistent sending schedule and frequency to keep your audience engaged and informed without overwhelming them with too many emails. Strike a balance between staying top-of-mind and respecting recipients' inbox space by sending emails at regular intervals and varying your content to keep it fresh and relevant.

10. Stay Innovative and Evolve

Embrace innovation and stay ahead of the curve by exploring new trends, technologies, and tactics in email marketing. Keep an eye on industry developments, competitor strategies, and emerging technologies to continuously evolve your approach and adapt to changing consumer preferences and behaviors.

By incorporating these lessons learned and best practices into your email marketing strategy, you can enhance the effectiveness of your campaigns, build stronger relationships with your audience, and achieve your business objectives more effectively in today's competitive digital landscape.

8.4 Building Your Email Marketing Strategy

Crafting a successful email marketing strategy requires careful planning, thoughtful execution, and ongoing optimization. Whether you're a large corporation or a small business, having a clear strategy in place is essential to achieving your goals and maximizing the impact of your email campaigns. Here's a step-by-step guide to building an effective email marketing strategy:

1. Define Your Objectives

Begin by defining clear and specific objectives for your email marketing efforts. Whether your goal is to drive sales, increase website traffic, generate leads, or build brand awareness, clearly outline what you aim to achieve with your email campaigns.

2. Know Your Audience

Understand your target audience's demographics, interests, preferences, and behaviors to tailor your email content and messaging effectively. Segment your audience based on relevant criteria to deliver personalized and relevant communications that resonate with recipients.

3. Choose the Right Email Marketing Platform

Select a reliable email marketing platform that aligns with your needs, budget, and technical requirements. Look for features such as customizable templates, automation capabilities, analytics tools, and scalability to support your email marketing strategy effectively.

4. Build Your Email List

Grow your email list organically by implementing opt-in strategies on your website, social media channels, and other touchpoints. Offer incentives such as exclusive content, discounts, or giveaways to encourage visitors to subscribe to your email list and stay engaged with your brand.

5. Create Compelling Content

Develop engaging and relevant content that resonates with your audience and aligns with your brand voice and values. Experiment with different content formats, such as newsletters, product announcements, educational resources, or promotional offers, to keep your emails fresh and engaging.

6. Optimize for Mobile Devices

Ensure that your emails are optimized for mobile viewing, as the majority of email opens occur on mobile devices. Use responsive design, clear formatting, and mobile-friendly calls-to-action to create a seamless and user-friendly experience for mobile users.

7. Implement Personalization

Utilize personalization tactics to tailor your email content and messaging to each recipient's preferences, past interactions, and purchase history. Incorporate dynamic content, merge tags, and segmentation strategies to deliver highly relevant and personalized communications that resonate with recipients.

8. Automate Workflows

Streamline your email marketing efforts by implementing automation workflows for tasks such as welcome emails, abandoned cart reminders, re-engagement campaigns, and lead nurturing sequences. Use automation tools to deliver timely and targeted messages based on recipient behavior and triggers.

9. Measure and Analyze Performance

Track key metrics such as open rates, click-through rates, conversion rates, and ROI to evaluate the performance of your email campaigns. Use analytics tools to gain insights into recipient behavior, identify areas for improvement, and optimize your strategies for better results.

10. Iterate and Improve

Continuously iterate and improve your email marketing strategy based on data-driven insights and feedback. Experiment with different tactics, test new ideas, and refine your approach over time to optimize performance, increase engagement, and achieve your objectives more effectively.

By following these steps and building a comprehensive email marketing strategy, you can enhance the effectiveness of your campaigns, build stronger relationships with your audience, and drive meaningful results for your business. Stay agile, stay innovative, and stay focused on delivering value to your subscribers to succeed in today's competitive email marketing landscape.

Conclusion

Email Marketing: A Comprehensive Guide to Strategies, Tips, and Best Practices for Effective Email Campaigns to Drive Sales, Build Relationships, Increase Sales, and Grow Your Business

In the fast-paced, ever-evolving digital landscape, email marketing remains a cornerstone strategy for businesses aiming to connect with their audience, drive sales, and foster long-term relationships. This comprehensive guide has taken you through the essential elements of crafting effective email campaigns, from understanding the fundamentals to exploring advanced techniques.

Recap of Key Insights

- **Understanding Email Marketing**: We began by defining email marketing and exploring its evolution and importance. Email marketing's ability to reach customers directly and personally makes it a powerful tool for businesses of all sizes.
- **Building a Quality Email List**: We delved into strategies for building and maintaining a high-quality email list. Understanding your audience, using effective opt-in methods, and adhering to ethical practices ensure a solid foundation for your campaigns.
- **Crafting Effective Email Content**: The importance of engaging subject lines, personalized content, and strategic visual design cannot be overstated. Tailoring your content to different campaign types helps maintain relevance and interest.
- **Designing and Sending Emails**: Creating responsive templates and optimizing for mobile devices is crucial for accessibility.

Proper scheduling and the use of email marketing tools enhance the delivery and impact of your messages.

- **Segmentation and Automation**: Segmenting your audience and automating workflows allow for more targeted and efficient communication. These strategies help deliver the right message to the right person at the right time.
- **Measuring and Analyzing Performance**: Tracking key metrics, conducting A/B testing, and analyzing campaign performance are vital for continuous improvement. Leveraging data-driven insights helps refine strategies and achieve better results.
- **Advanced Strategies and Integration**: Integrating email with other channels, leveraging AI, and utilizing interactive content are advanced tactics that can significantly boost engagement. Staying ahead of trends ensures your email marketing remains effective.
- **Case Studies and Practical Examples**: Learning from successful campaigns of both leading brands and small businesses provides valuable inspiration and practical takeaways for your efforts.

The Path Forward

Email marketing is more than just a communication tool; it's a dynamic platform for building relationships, nurturing leads, and driving conversions. As you move forward, remember these key principles:

- **Customer-Centric Approach**: Always prioritize the needs and preferences of your audience. Personalized, relevant, and value-driven content fosters trust and loyalty.
- **Continuous Learning and Adaptation**: Stay informed about industry trends, emerging technologies, and changing consumer

behaviors. Adapt your strategies to remain competitive and effective.

- **Innovation and Experimentation**: Don't be afraid to try new ideas and innovative approaches. Experimentation leads to insights that can significantly enhance your campaigns.
- **Ethical Practices and Compliance**: Adhering to ethical standards and regulatory requirements builds credibility and ensures long-term success.

Final Thoughts

The journey through email marketing is one of constant evolution and adaptation. By applying the strategies, tips, and best practices outlined in this guide, you're equipped to create impactful email campaigns that not only drive sales but also build lasting relationships with your audience.

Remember, the true power of email marketing lies in its ability to connect with individuals on a personal level, delivering messages that resonate and inspire action. As you implement and refine your email marketing efforts, keep your focus on delivering value, fostering engagement, and nurturing trust.

Thank you for joining us on this comprehensive exploration of email marketing. May your campaigns be successful, your audience engaged, and your business growth unstoppable. Happy emailing!

www.ingramcontent.com/pod-product-compliance
Lightning Source LLC
Chambersburg PA
CBHW082108220526
45472CB00009B/2094